Harvard Business School Career Guide

Finance 1994

In Cooperation with the
Harvard Business School
Finance Club

Edited by

Alan S. Axelrod
Paul D. Horvath

Harvard Business School
Class of 1994

Distributed by the
Harvard Business School Press

ISBN 0-87584-427-8
ISSN 0899-7098

Contents

Firms Describe Themselves: Finance

Preface

This is the second edition of the *Harvard Business School Career Guide: Finance*, produced by the Harvard Business School Finance Club and distributed by the Harvard Business School Press. It is a continuation of the series *Harvard Business School Career Guide: Investment Banking*, produced by the Baker Library Career Resources Center. In addition to descriptions of investment banks that have been profiled in previous editions, this book contains descriptions of many other firms, including commercial banks, *Fortune* 500 companies, and regional firms that recruit MBAs for positions in finance.

The purpose of this guide is to assist readers in their job search by presenting profiles of the numerous companies that recruit MBAs for finance positions. The guide describes the different positions, career paths, and lifestyles, as well as the recruiting process, at each of these firms.

Professors Samuel L. Hayes III and Joshua Lerner of Harvard Business School share their insights about careers in finance, and two 1993 graduates from the Harvard Business School—one with experience in an investment bank and another who pursued a finance career in a *Fortune* 500 company—report candidly on their experiences there and describe what job seekers can expect. Additional alumni perspectives are provided by three seasoned HBS graduates who are well-accomplished in their particular finance fields and who share some of their experiences and secrets to success. Also included in the guide are a mailing list of contacts for the companies described in the guide, a helpful glossary of finance terms, and a selective bibliography of relevant books and directories compiled by Sue Marsh, the Harvard Business School Career Resources Librarian.

We thank the people at the various firms who contributed to this book. In addition, many thanks go to Professors Samuel L. Hayes III and Joshua Lerner, Anne Liang, Brian Webber, Seth Rosenblatt, Vikram Gandhi, Girish Nadkarni, Joel Peterson, and Alistair Williamson for all of their help in preparing this book.

ALAN S. AXELROD,
LOS ANGELES, AUGUST 1993

PAUL D. HORVATH
BUDAPEST, AUGUST 1993

Introduction

Samuel L. Hayes III
Jacob H. Schiff Professor of Investment Banking
Harvard Business School

Joshua Lerner
Assistant Professor
Harvard Business School

Business school faculty have many occasions to counsel students gearing up for the post-MBA job market. It is, to be sure, a time of high expectations. At the same time, the post-MBA job search can be daunting, even for those who have been through a search before.

Identifying and landing a job in the field of finance presents many of the same challenges of other functional areas: identifying promising potential employers, evaluating and discriminating among various job possibilities, assessing the long-term potential of a particular entry-level job, and so forth. At the same time, a finance job search poses certain special challenges. This book will give you a head start in the investigatory "due diligence" effort we all go through in the course of a job campaign.

The word *financial* in a job description usually reveals very little about the work content. One business school student took a summer job between the first and second years of his MBA program that seemed to promise opportunities for financial analysis within a large corporation. He had in mind the sort of strategic decision-making process that had dominated his first-year finance course. The actual job content turned out to be bread-and-butter accounting. Thankfully, the job was only temporary; he gamely did the work as competently as possible and then gracefully withdrew at the end of the summer.

Although it is difficult to categorize financial jobs, they can be broken down into those that take place within a corporate organization and those whose setting is a particular financial institution. The structure of finance functions within a corporation is easier to articulate. Typically, there is a chief financial officer (CFO) under whom internal financial (controllership) and external financial (treasurer) activities are grouped. In many companies, strategic and long-range planning have considerable finance content and may also report to the CFO, if only on a dotted-line basis.

Jobs concerned with the collection, measurement, and evaluation of financial data generated from internal operations are typically placed under the controller's super-

vision. In these jobs, training in accounting (and possibly auditing) comes in very handy. An organization's relations with financial markets and institutions are often grouped under the supervision of the treasurer. These include management of bank lines and other credit facilities to ensure that the company can pay its bills in a timely fashion, communication with shareholders, and oversight of offshore financing arrangements. (The increasing frequency of foreign activities reflects the growing integration of national economies into a large, interdependent global market.) Evaluation of external acquisitions, or the sale of parts of the company's own operations, could be grouped under the treasurer's umbrella or within a separate office.

Most ambitious MBA graduates are eager to be at the heart of the real action in a company. In many ways, this is what they have been trained for. If you are of this disposition, it is important to determine the center of financial action within a prospective employer.

Many graduating MBAs are immediately attracted to the treasury function and to strategic financial planning. These seem glamorous and represent activities that are closely related to the newly minted MBAs' training. In some companies, primarily those serving essentially as holding companies for a number of decentralized operating units, the financial focus may be on the company's relations with external capital markets. But despite the glitz associated with strategic planning and the treasurer's contacts with Wall Street and other external organizations, the real guts of the financial function for most firms—the site of the real action—is internal control.

Among financial vendors—commercial banks, investment banks, insurance companies, and money management firms—the array of job possibilities is extremely broad:

Corporate finance
Investment analysis
Portfolio management
Trading
Institutional and retail sales
"Financial engineering," or the application of
   quantitative methods to the construction of
   financial products
General management

Corporate finance in the context of a financial vendor typically involves the basket of products, services, and counsel marketed to nonfinancial companies. This is an

1

elastic definition. For investment banks, it encompasses the structuring and issuance of new securities to the public. For finance companies, such as GE Credit, corporate finance has a different meaning. GE Credit does not itself underwrite securities but does offer a broad variety of services to corporate customers, including secured financing and general counsel on corporate financial strategy.

Investment analysis is usually associated with the role of the analyst of publicly traded securities. Typically focusing on only one category of securities (e.g., the auto industry, "junk" bonds), analysts are employed by many different vendors. These may be on either the buy side (investment management firms or other institutional investors such as insurance companies and pension managers) or the sell side (securities firms and commercial banks). Sell-side analysts typically focus on products that they and their institutional sales colleagues think can be sold to portfolio managers responsible for the investment of large pools of savings. Buy-side analysts generally play the role of thoughtful skeptics in evaluating ideas generated by vendor firms.

Portfolio managers are often veteran security analysts, although some vendors hire young people for direct assignment as portfolio managers. Some portfolio managers describe their field as the place "where the buck stops." While the analyst recommends actions on certain securities, the portfolio manager makes the ultimate decisions and is evaluated on the consequences.

If portfolio managers are under the gun to demonstrate quarter-by-quarter quality performance, traders of particular categories of stocks, bonds, and derivatives live minute-by-minute. The consequences of their judgments are usually priced out each day for everyone to see. This is an exciting, "white-knuckle" business that attracts certain types of personalities.

Institutional sales people work closely with traders and security analysts and create a bridge between them and the big institutions whose investment activities dominate modern public markets. They sell products that their firms have either developed or acquired for resale, and they must be conversant with the details of these products and how they serve the objectives of their institutional customers. The days of the "gentleman bond salesman" immortalized by F. Scott Fitzgerald are long gone. This is a demanding business—and the rewards for success are extraordinary.

Retail securities sales involves the marketing of stocks, bonds, and other financial products to individual investors. These investors are, on the average, likely to be less sophisticated than institutional investors and therefore are dependent on their brokers for more comprehensive counsel. Building a retail customer base takes time, but these customers tend to be loyal to their individual brokers and often follow them if they move from one brokerage house to another in search of a more lucrative deal or better support. Retail brokerage is one of the last bastions of relationship-based financial business.

Derivative securities—the disaggregation and reconstruction of securities with features specifically tailored to particular types of investors or issues—have become big business for some financial vendors and their clients. For vendors possessing the proprietary quantitative techniques used to construct and price out these hybrid securities, derivatives have been very profitable.

Jobs focusing on the *management* of financial service firms have gotten much more attention in recent years. More than a decade of acquisitions, mergers, and internally generated growth has made these firms larger and more complex; they no longer lend themselves to the informal managerial oversight long characteristic of the business. Back-office jobs are a case in point. After a variety of securities vendors became overloaded by the trading volume in the late 1960s and 1970s, the firms' leadership realized that the fate of their organizations was tied to their ability to get their internal paperwork and controls better organized. This change has raised the stature of professionals opting for internal management careers. Similarly, commercial banks discovered that a secret to successful expansion and profitability in the contemporary marketplace lies in the management of their own information systems. John Reed, CEO of Citibank, owes his leadership post, at least in part, to his successful mastery of this area.

It should be cautioned, however, that many general managers of financial service organizations have come up through the ranks as specialists in a product or service rather than through an initial career entry into the vendor's internal management structure. Many of these organizations still hold the highest places of honor for top business getters and revenue producers. However, an appreciation for professional management skills is gradually developing.

Students seeking to enter the finance profession must grapple with several challenging decisions. A crucial issue is whether finance is the right occupation. A finance career almost invariably involves long hours, stress, and often great uncertainty. If the field itself does not genuinely excite you or stimulate your curiosity, it is unlikely to be a happy choice, no matter how generous the compensation.

The next question is the appropriate subfields of finance on which to focus the job search. The demands of various subfields vary considerably. Some areas, such as trading and selling complex derivative securities, place a premium on quantitative abilities. In others, such as retail brokerage, the ability to communicate clearly and persuasively is paramount. The time demands of these positions also vary considerably. For instance, while corporate finance demands a considerable amount of time—to the point of serious conflicts between family and work—trading positions have traditionally been less demanding from an hours-per-week perspective.

A third decision relates to the institutions on which to focus job-searching efforts. Each organization has a distinctive personality. Finding a good match between an employer's personality and your own is an important prerequisite to long-run success. The descriptions contained in this book and the promotional material you will receive during the interviewing process should provide some indication of these firm-by-firm differences. Important insights can also be gathered through conversations with peers who have worked or are currently working for these organizations. But ultimately it is very difficult for others to point you toward the best match; it is a personal choice and an issue to which you should be particularly sensitive during the interviewing process.

Concerning the job search itself, several thoughts may be helpful. One frequent source of concern of students relates to the résumé. What résumé features, students wonder, will pique the interest of a financial services vendor? How do you avoid either overselling or underselling your credentials? How should the "job objective" section be handled? Although there is no single answer to these questions, among the key things potential employers look for is evidence of your purpose and direction. Do you appreciate the demands of the position that you are seeking? Do you understand the characteristics of the firm that you are pursuing? Are you serious about a finance career, or is this just one more option along with consulting, marketing, and other industries? The importance of thorough preparation for the job search process cannot be overestimated. This same concern applies to the interview process, only more so.

The successful completion of a job search is just a beginning. To translate the promise of a new job into long-run success requires the same careful thought and planning that won the job. A sure prerequisite is unmistakable enthusiasm for the work, which manifests itself as energy and personal innovation.

As you take your first position, be aware of several pitfalls that have derailed promising careers. The first relates to workload. Finance jobs tend to be high pressure and demand long hours. Giving the job the best you have is essential. But it is also necessary to pace yourself and ensure that the office does not entirely dominate your life. Without outside interests and time to enjoy them, it will be only a question of when, not if, you burn out.

A second mistake can be to move too quickly toward specialization. One objective of your initial position should be to illuminate the variety of potential career opportunities. Limiting your early career experience to a narrow focus on a particular product or a single industry, for instance, may limit your ability to move on to other opportunities as they present themselves.

A final point concerns the very nature of "opportunities." Our natural tendency, when faced with an uncertain future, is to plan our way out of it. But developing too precise a plan, and sticking rigidly to it, is likely to be a mistake. Career opportunities have a way of surfacing when one least expects them. Be alert for new and unanticipated opportunities that will almost surely come along. As Disraeli warned, "What we anticipate seldom comes; what we least expected generally happens."

Good luck!

Jobs in Investment Banking

Seth A. Rosenblatt

Harvard Business School, Class of 1993
Vice President, Finance Club

What Is Investment Banking?

Investment banking denotes and connotes a number of different ideas. For those who have not worked in the industry before and are considering a summer or full-time position in investment banking, the job search can bring confusion and frustration.

In a very general sense, the term *investment bank* is broadly used to describe any financial institution that provides services in the areas of security issuing and brokering, financial advisory, or asset management. From the smallest boutiques to the large full-service firms, the term *investment bank* is far too often used. Large investment banks such as the "bulge-bracket" firms engage in many arenas outside traditional commercial banking or insurance underwriting. However, the function of investment banking requires a narrower industry definition. Investment banking generally encompasses four functions, all interrelated. Some firms may engage in all of these functions, while some may specialize in one or more of these areas:

1. Corporate finance.

2. Mergers and acquisitions.

3. Merchant banking.

4. Advisory/financial consulting.

In addition, many firms may specialize in one or two industry groups. The largest firms tend to have many functional and/or industry groups to serve their client base fully. Although many of the terms used here are fairly universal, the terminology in different countries does vary. If you are looking for an investment banking job outside the United States, become familiar with specific terminology used there (exact translations do not necessarily apply).

Corporate Finance

Corporate finance is the process of raising money for corporate clients (or public institutions) in the form of equity, debt, convertible, or other derivative security. This process involves two steps: (1) determining the funding needs of the client (type, amount, and structure) and (2) finding investors to supply those funds. This second step can generally be accomplished through either of two methods: a public issue or a private placement. A public issuance of a security involves the investment bank's acting as an underwriter of the securities, purchasing the securities from the issuer and then reselling them on the public market. For larger investment banks, this process will involve other areas of the firm, such as sales and trading, research, and a syndicate function (sharing the underwriting responsibilities with other investment banks). A private placement, on the other hand, calls for the investment bank to act solely as an agent, matching the issuer of the security with one or a handful of potential investors in an offering not made available to the public.

Mergers and Acquisitions

For investment bankers the much publicized "M&A" business has the banker acting as an advisor to a company in transactions involving the sale of a whole company, a division, or just certain assets. The investment banker acts as an advisor to the client (on either the buy side or sell side), determines an appropriate valuation range, and negotiates terms most favorable to the client. The investment bank may also take a more active role by participating as a principal in the transaction. From an auction to a negotiated sale, from a stock swap to an LBO, the form and structure of an M&A transaction vary widely.

Merchant Banking

Merchant banking is the process whereby an investment bank acts as a principal in a transaction, either by purchasing newly issued securities of a firm or by purchasing (or selling) a stake in an M&A transaction. Some firms specialize only in merchant banking, while the largest investment banks tend to have a separate group to perform this function. Merchant banking is closely tied to the functions of corporate finance and M&A, and bankers from different industry or functional groups normally work on a merchant banking transaction together.

Advisory

Advisory work is linked to corporate finance, M&A, and merchant banking. It is generally performed as part of the overall service given to clients, or it may be tied to a specific transaction. Advisory or consulting work can take an infinite number of forms, including capital structure analysis, comparable analysis, and industry research. Much of the specific work is dependent on the particular client's industry. In addition, the past few years have seen a dramatic growth in advisory work related to corporate restructurings and reorganizations.

Looking for a Job in Investment Banking

For those who have not previously worked in the industry, a lot of anxiety arises in the investment banking job search. For first-year students who are seriously considering making a career switch into investment banking, I strongly recommend that you work in the field for the summer. Not only will this make it easier to find a job with an investment bank after your second year, but you will learn what the industry is all about. Investment banking is such a unique field that it is difficult to understand the work, the environment, and the culture without experiencing it.

When beginning your self-assessment and your job search, first speak to as many people as you can who are or have been in the industry. In your class, you will probably find at least a dozen people who worked in an investment bank for at least two years. Your peers will be your greatest resource. Ask a lot of questions; you will get a good cross-section of various experiences, good and bad.

Many of your business school classmates have been former "analysts." *Analyst* is the usual entry-level title for undergraduates. Understand, that if hired, you will probably enter at the associate level (or equivalent). Although the long hours may be similar, the responsibilities may be very different. Try to understand the general career path in investment banking and the specific one in each firm.

Your next stops should be at the placement center and the library. Try to research each firm in which you may be interested. Understand which firms are full-service broker-dealers and investment bankers, which are middle-market firms, and which are boutiques. What appears to be the corporate culture and reputation of each firm? Does a firm specialize in a particular industry, function, or geographic region? Does it match your interests? Try to discover, through speaking with peers and research, which firms are the leaders in each of the areas (industries or functions) in which you are interested. There are a number of specific places where you can look for information on each firm that you are researching. Your career resource center will have the following information:

- Annual reports, 10-Ks, 10-Qs, prospectuses (if it is a public company)
- Recruiting brochures
- Company files
- Industry file/packet
- Summer job reports
- Current and previous job descriptions
- Lotus One Source/Other online services
- Alumni career advisor list
- Book of job search and salary statistics

Additionally, check these sources:
- Company recruiting briefings and dinners
- *Wall Street Journal*
- Business magazines (*BusinessWeek*, *Forbes*, *Fortune*, *Economist*)
- LEXIS/NEXIS news searches (available on-line)
- Job Search Guide (available from your career center)
- Career fairs
- Friends, relatives, classmates, professors
- This book

Most of the larger investment banking firms, although they may have offices throughout the country and the rest of the world, tend to be based in New York City and do all recruiting from there. Regardless of which office you may be interested in, you may have to go through a general interviewing process based in New York. Be sure to understand each firm's policies and procedures for hiring outside the main office, particularly internationally. Many firms have a bias toward hiring nationals of a particular country to work in an office located there. If you are unsure, ask. During the correspondence and interviewing process, make your geographic preferences clear. If you can work only in city X, you will find it very frustrating to go through the entire process and be offered a job, only to find that the firm is not hiring this year in city X. Try to understand office placement policies before the interview.

Attend as many recruiting briefings as you can to get an idea of each firm's strategy, focus, and culture. Compare the people who have been successful in each firm to your own track record and where (or who) you would like to be in 5, 10, or 20 years. Finally, make it a practice to read the newspaper (the *Wall Street Journal* in particular) to get a good sense of what is going on in the industry and with specific firms.

If you have done sufficient researching and querying, the interview should be the easiest part of the process. These interviews are generally not like "stress" consulting interviews. You will probably not be asked the implications of an inverted yield curve or queried as to the number of restaurants in New York City. This, of course, varies by firm (and there are stories of difficult interviews), but in general investment banks are looking to see if you:

- Are a hard worker and detail oriented.

- Have leadership skills and enjoy working in groups.

- Have a genuine interest in the industry and are excited about it.

- Show good judgment and demonstrate responsibility.

- Are analytically inclined and comfortable with numbers and computers.

- Understand the lifestyle and are willing to make the sacrifices required.

- Are a fun person to be around. ("Would I like to go to dinner with you?")

Conclusion

You must determine what methods of research work best for you. Speak to people whose advice you value, and then draw your own conclusions. Two issues that need to be addressed are the money and the hours. Much time has been spent talking about both of these subjects.

All in all, I found investment banking to be a great experience. It was stimulating and challenging, and I got to work with some fascinating people. If you decide to make a career of it, do it for reasons like this. If you find, through talking to peers or through a summer job, that you do not expect to get the same kind of fun, challenge,

or excitement that I did, do not go into the industry. You will be miserable. Investment banking is not for everybody. Where I worked, there were a few of my peers who thought that it was the greatest experience of their lives, while others, doing the exact same job, were miserable. In other words, the money should *not* be the deciding factor. There is little doubt that investment banking is one of the best-paying positions (in the short run) that you can take, and money is certainly not unimportant. Although compensation is always a consideration in any job decision, the people I knew who regretted the job the most were the ones who took it solely for the cash.

As for the hours, this is something also that has sparked quite a legend on Wall Street—and throughout the rest of the business world. Stories of all-nighters and ruined weekends plague the minds of former analysts. While it is true that investment bankers work very long hours, the variance within and among firms is so large that it defies most generalizations. Nevertheless, there usually is some lifestyle sacrifice that particularly a junior banker will have to make in investment banking. The only way to get an accurate sense of the hours is for you to talk to friends or classmates who worked for a particular firm. Even then, their information may not be accurate because different departments in the same firm may require much different hours. Additionally, changes in the business cycle and season can dramatically affect the work load in any firm.

Only through asking a lot of questions and through a little soul searching can you determine if the investment banking lifestyle is indeed right for you.

Finance Careers in Manufacturing Companies

Brian M. Webber

Harvard Business School, Class of 1993
Co-President, Finance Club

A variety of career opportunities is available to students interested in finance other than well-known financial services jobs. Manufacturing companies have positions in strategic planning, product development, and division controllers' offices. I worked as a financial analyst in product development at Ford Motor Company prior to attending HBS.

In the controller's office of product development, I worked on various product development teams associated with the development of new models of Taurus and Sable. Product development teams consist of engineers, marketing people, planning people, and a finance person. My main responsibility was to perform the financial analysis required by the team when making product decisions, but I was also exposed to a wide array of team decisions and problems and to the team strategies and solutions employed throughout the development process. I met daily with team members to review, update, and discuss the progress of the new product. The requirements of this assignment were to visit the plants of small suppliers, assist with cost control and financial projections, and work closely with development engineers and designers to report the financial status of the program to senior management. Since each team member is encouraged to contribute and to assume responsibility where feasible, I quickly gained a reasonable knowledge of the entire development process. Interaction with engineering, marketing, planning, and outside suppliers was extremely interesting and helped me to understand the engineering and marketing functions. Often the various functional areas are faced with conflicting goals, and compromises among team members are required. Frequently team meetings are held at supplier locations, where the team analyzes specific product proposals, or meetings are held in the prototype plant next to a prototype vehicle so that decisions can be implemented in real time. Finance positions in product development allow a finance person to work closely with the manufacturing process. Every member of the product development team provides input for decisions that affect the outcome of the product.

The environment in product development finance is intense, and the hours are demanding. The hours do not compare to investment banking hours but are considerably longer than other positions within the company. A great deal of responsibility is heaped on finance representatives with respect to

reporting to senior management the financial status of the new product, preparing financial models to analyze the impact of various proposals, and assuming team leadership at times when financial analysis has a major impact on a product decision. Analysts may also evaluate future marketing programs and compare competitors' products from a financial perspective. Analysts perform business analyses for new programs that include profitability, return on capital, evaluation of alternatives, and presentations to senior management.

Product development is only one aspect of finance within a manufacturing company. Other areas requiring financial expertise are sales and marketing, capital markets, and manufacturing.

Sales and marketing finance positions require analysts to evaluate and develop appropriate strategies for retail pricing and various incentive programs. With recent developments in automobile pricing, such as cash back and low interest financing, a great deal of analysis is required to recommend appropriate pricing levels. Analysts also evaluate competitors' pricing strategies and form arguments for an appropriate counterresponse.

Capital markets finance positions exist both within credit areas, such as Ford Motor Credit, and in various treasury areas. Analysts provide financial support for issuance of commercial paper, long-term debt, common and preferred stock, and sale leaseback transactions. Analysts act as buyers of various investment banking services. Analysts recommend strategies for capital structure and dividend policies, manage daily cash flow, and perform analyses for acquisitions and divestitures.

Manufacturing finance positions involve developing capital budgets and analyzing specific capital spending projects. Analysts are involved with site analysis and evaluate new plant proposals. They also analyze financial and operating results of manufacturing plants.

A finance background can often open doors for international assignments depending on the size and needs of the company. Many of my colleagues planned to work internationally, and I saw doors open up for them to do so.

There are many things to consider when choosing a summer job or a career, including location and corporate environment. The best source of information is often individuals who have worked in the industry or have worked for the specific company you are considering. Do not hesitate to contact someone who has worked for a company or in an area you are considering.

Interviews: Three Harvard Business School Alumni Reflect on Careers in Finance

Vikram Gandhi

Harvard Business School, Class of 1989
Senior Associate, Mergers and Acquisitions
Morgan Stanley & Company

Describe the stages of your career path and changes in responsibility.

During the first couple of years, my career developed along a diversified set of experiences. I worked in Capital Markets, the Natural Resource Area, and the Merger and Acquisitions/Restructuring Area. These two years served as a time to build a network of relationships and access pockets of knowledge throughout the firm. In addition to being exposed to new functional and industry arenas, this stage enabled me to develop and refine my teamwork skills further. My role was primarily to complete modules of a large project and to contribute to the team's efforts in executing transactions.

The opportunity to move around in the first two years was a valuable experience for two reasons. First, given the nature of the investment banking industry and flux of the business, you should not expect to have a "home" for good, and so it is worthwhile to share in multiple experiences in case you need to shift specialties in the future. Second, given the importance of working with a variety of people, the more people you meet, the better you will be positioned later in your career.

My first two years emphasized agenda execution; my current career stage emphasizes agenda setting as a team manager in the M&A group. I now work more directly with the principals and managing directors, am responsible for ensuring the quality of the team's work, and manage analysts and new associates. A critical junction in my role as team manager is to manage upward and across specialty areas to ensure that the necessary expertise is brought to bear to solve client problems.

What have been the obstacles and challenges of your career progression?

Three challenges in my career have been managing up, coordinating resources, and motivating down. First, since I am now responsible for ensuring the quality of work yet lack many years of experience, it is imperative that I seek the perspective of senior people, and getting their time is not easy. Therefore, it is critical to get them to focus, and one must manage and communicate effectively to accomplish this feat.

Second, a key success factor in investment banking is bringing various resources of the firm to bear on a project. This requires a healthy dose of coordination, especially since I work on six to seven projects at a time. Achieving cooperation in a firm with many egos is a challenge. One must massage egos when coordinating to ensure that what colleagues and senior people say is intelligently articulated to the client.

A third challenge is motivating down. We work hard at Morgan Stanley, and it is vital to maintain a good experience for the analysts and new associates. I must position the work as a valuable and fun experience so that junior people do not mind being at work until 1 A.M. I need to motivate them so they feel involved and they have a high degree of job satisfaction.

Can you describe an experience that has significantly influenced your career?

I enjoy my job, but I cannot point to any one experience that has significantly influenced my career.

What strengths have helped you excel in your career?

A strength that has helped me in my career is being analytically oriented. This should come as no big surprise, but it is especially relevant to M&A given the abundance of valuation and creative structuring required. Another strength is being involved in many extracurricular activities while at school. This involvement was valuable for enabling me to obtain a better understanding of how people think and work. The key to success at Morgan Stanley is teamwork, and my extracurricular activities enhanced my ability to manage my time, to motivate, and to keep people interested in what they are doing while getting the most out of them.

Where do you see your career going over the next ten years? How will you prepare for such changes?

I'm happy in investment banking. I enjoy what I do because it builds on my strengths, and there is a fair degree of variety in the projects I work on. Yes, investment banking is tiring and difficult, but it's also fun. Hence, I'd like to continue for at least the next few years as I transition from a team manager to a team leader. Yet over the long haul, I can see myself getting involved on the principal side of the business.

To prepare for the future, I focus on my interactions with senior firm officials and senior client officials. Eventually, it will be important for me to secure clients if I hope to transition to a team leader. Therefore, I make sure I know current clients well and build those relationships while establishing others. Preparing for the future means that when a client has a problem, he or she will call on me.

To what extent did your HBS degree prepare you for the day-to-day life of Morgan Stanley?

HBS definitely prepares you for investment banking. One works on six to seven projects at a time in different industries, and the work requires creative problem solving. At Morgan Stanley, I might be considering a joint venture for a natural resource client, a buying opportunity for an auto client, and a selling opportunity for a telecommunications client. This might be only half of the projects on my plate at any given time. And like HBS, even though I had less time to think about the business situation, I would have to grasp key issues of three business situations each evening. So, similar to the requirements for being an exceptional investment banker, HBS prepares one to handle a lot of stuff in a short amount of time and effectively deal with the intensity of work.

The second way HBS prepared me was in the exercise of analytics. Every day I have to go through thick documents or consider complicated situations and come up with three key issues. The client describes a problem, and it's my job to figure out some options and decide which makes the most sense for the client. This type of work is not too different from discussions that occurred every day in Aldrich Hall.

Finally, a third way that HBS prepared me was with regard to people. The people at HBS are the same type that I work with at Morgan Stanley; they're smart and hard working, but they often have large egos. HBS prepared me well for those types of people.

Is there anything else you would recommend to future HBS graduates entering the finance industry?

First, teamwork is critical to success and should not be underestimated. HBS makes some people think they can be a solo star, but it just doesn't work that way.

Second, don't try to run before you can walk. Coming out of HBS, you may think there's not much more to learn. Nothing could be further from the truth. A place like Morgan Stanley can humble you. Consider your first couple of years as an opportunity where you are being paid to learn. I strongly recommend that you demonstrate an eagerness to learn.

Third, recognize that investment banking is a cyclical industry. You must anticipate that while today the equity product might be hot while M&A is slow, the situation could reverse itself very quickly. Given this industry nature, you should be flexible to change as it may become necessary to shift to different industry or function groups during your career. But the good thing to remember is that the HBS education enables you to be flexible because of the exposure to many industries, functions, people, and business situations.

Girish V. Nadkarni

Harvard Business School, Class of 1988
Vice President, Strategic Transactions
The Prudential Insurance Company of America

Describe the stages of your career path and changes in responsibility.

Before attending HBS, I practiced law on Wall Street: three years with Coudert Brothers and three years with Shearman & Sterling. Hence, my first job after HBS is not typical for MBAs straight out of school. After graduating from HBS, I was hired as Vice President and Assistant to the Vice Chairman of The Prudential Insurance Co. of America, responsible for handling a variety of special projects for the Vice Chairman. I also was "on loan" to the heads of several business units throughout The Prudential. The work I was assigned often pertained to strategic initiatives and gave me wide exposure to Prudential's businesses. For instance, one of the special projects required me to work on a task force to assess the sensitivity of Prudential's leveraged buyout (LBO) portfolio to recession.

Fourteen months later, I was promoted to Corporate Vice President in the Central Financial Services Group of Prudential Capital Corporation, responsible for new product development. One of the products I created was Pru-Shelf, a proprietary medium-term note program. Our first Pru-Shelf transaction was a $200 million financing with Toys R Us. To date, The Prudential has executed approximately 24 Pru-Shelf transactions totaling $1.6 billion. The product was featured in articles in *Corporate*

Finance, *Investment Dealer's Digest*, and *Investors Daily* and was also included in a *Business Week* cover story on innovative financial instruments. I also led a team that helped Prudential Capital's 14 regional offices manage complex transactions, such as LBOs and cashouts.

In 1990, I transferred to the work-out area of Prudential Capital and assumed a portfolio of 16 troubled companies. No other job has stretched me so much physically, emotionally, and intellectually. Every day was a crisis. Extensive negotiating and posturing skills were critical in this job, and when I was reassigned to my current position 18 months later, I knew my strengths and weaknesses.

For a number of reasons that range from Hurricane Andrew to the new risk-based capital requirements imposed on insurance companies, The Prudential has embarked on a reassessment of its main lines of business. Consequently, in my current position as Vice President, Strategic Transactions with the Prudential Investment Corporation, I help with the strategic assessment of different businesses and carry out the decisions to eliminate or expand a business unit. If we decide to expand a business or acquire companies, then I might lead an effort to raise external capital. If, on the other hand, we decide to exit a business, then I will execute a sale of our operations in that business.

What have been the obstacles and challenges of your career progression?

I have faced three challenges: diversity, politics, and a line versus staff trade-off. I was born and raised in India and therefore am different from most of the other people at The Prudential. I have independent opinions, and I tend to state them. There is the natural challenge of being different from the status quo and the challenge of peers resisting someone like me who does not always agree with their decisions, analyses, and opinions.

Entering an organization at a high level has its own challenges. People often resent you for not having paid your dues. It therefore takes a lot of effort and time to establish your credibility.

I also have been challenged by my lack of roots to a home unit within The Prudential. This has come about because of my constant transfers from one area of the company to another—wherever the action is hot. I'm not really complaining, though, because putting out fires has been exciting. But movements between line and staff positions can be difficult. It's especially hard to move back into a line assignment after having been in a staff position. But,

unfortunately, I am not considered part of the family by any group or senior person and there is no one other than myself who looks after my career.

Can you describe an experience that has significantly influenced your career?

Our business is fraught with legal issues; if we take the wrong step, we'll be sued. And though I am not trained in bankruptcy law, my legal background provides me with the ability to understand most of the intricacies of the work-out business. I also know how to make the most of our own lawyers. In fact, because of my legal experience, the synergy between our legal counsel and me is fantastic. Between us, we make one and one equals six.

A second significant experience is my assignment in the work-out area, where I honed my negotiating skills and learned and practiced the art of diplomacy, often facing people with diverging interests and constantly shifting alliances. I developed a better understanding of finance and strengthened my structuring skills. And I achieved better credit analysis as I saw what can and does go wrong in companies. I also learned that you cannot underestimate the critical need and value for good management and should not analyze a company without considering the probable significant changes imminent within the industry.

What strengths have helped you excel in your career?

My legal background has been a remarkable strength. Another strength is my generalist experience at The Prudential. Although it sometimes hurts not to have a home, transferring throughout the organization has given me wide exposure and a holistic view of Prudential's business. It also taught me to get up to speed quickly. The problems with diversity are synthesizing experiences that will make me an excellent senior manager in the long run. Other strengths include creative problem solving, structuring, and negotiating skills.

Where do you see your career going over the next ten years? How will you prepare for such changes?

I honestly have no clue where my career will be in ten years. The Prudential is experiencing a major transition. Its business is already very different than it was just five years ago. Uncertainty is a big problem. Like most other Harvard Business School alumni, I wouldn't mind being on my own one day, maybe with my own fund. And perhaps unlike most other HBS alumni, I have a strong interest in politics and am likely to run for some type of office one day. The future is definitely uncertain but exciting.

Preparing for uncertainty is a challenge. Often it's not what you know that is important but who you know. It is very important to know the right people—those who make the decisions and not those who make the most noise. It is valuable to adopt a mentor and build credibility.

To what extent did your HBS degree prepare you for the day-to-day life of The Prudential?

I loved my two years at HBS. They gave me tremendous analytical and problem-solving capabilities, as well as frameworks and paradigms to guide my thinking. The education forced me to understand the economics of a business. I graduated appreciating that there are times when the process of making decisions is more important than the substance; that achieving commitment, involvement, and organizational buy-in is not easy; that getting the rank and file to adopt and implement plans is about applying the right process; and that treating customers and employees well is critical to survival.

Nevertheless, HBS failed to prepare me for many of the soft issues that one deals with every day. Perhaps I wasn't listening, but it didn't teach me how to manage my career in a political organization. HBS taught me how to manage others but not how to be managed. It's like expecting one to be a parent before he or she has finished being a child. Furthermore, HBS fell short of enabling me to handle entering an organization at a high-profile level and to fight the stereotypes of an "HBS Baker Scholar type."

Is there anything else you would recommend to future HBS graduates entering the finance industry?

First, make sure you know why you want to be in finance. Too many people think it's a stepping-stone to bigger and better things. For instance, many people think investment banking or mergers and acquisitions is a stepping-stone to running your own business one day. Nothing in investment banking prepares you for running your own business. If you want to operate a business, then consider marketing. Investment banking teaches one only how to process transactions. Make sure you know what working life will be like on a day-to-day basis. Don't choose money management because you want your photograph in the newspaper as the next Peter Lynch. Make sure you understand what Peter Lynch did at Fidelity on a daily basis.

Know your strengths and play to them, and don't forget soft issues both inside and outside your company. Remember that judgment is more important than technical skills. It's critical to reach a judgment based on what the numbers say and not just crunch them. Don't hesitate to push the envelope. Too many people think they are pushing the envelope, but often they don't know where the envelope really is, or they define it too narrowly. Finally, to succeed at the top, it's helpful to be a generalist. Yet there's a trade-off, because to get to the top you need to be a specialist and the risk is obsolescence of your specialty; so be careful to follow industry dynamics constantly, and if they change, manage your career accordingly.

Joel W. Peterson

Harvard Business School, Class of 1983
Managing Director, Utilities
CIBC, a subsidiary of Canadian Imperial Bank of Commerce

Describe the stages of your career path and changes in responsibility.

I would describe my career in five stages: the Learning Stage, "Just Another Banker" Stage, "Not Just Another Banker" Stage, People Manager Stage, and "Not Just Another Manager" Stage.

> *The Learning Stage* (about one year): This is the period right after business school, when I tried to absorb as much information as possible, figure out who's who, and simply do my best even though I was not sure what specific career benefit would accrue from a particular work matter.
> *"Just Another Banker" Stage* (about two years): In this stage I sought valuable personal contacts and team-building opportunities. I knew enough to be dangerous yet not enough to be noticed or have too much impact.
> *"Not Just Another Banker" Stage* (about three years): At this point in my career, I had real impact. This was manifested in specific transactions in which I could differentiate myself through personal excellence and organizational team-building skills.
> *People Manager Stage* (about two years): Although I have always managed projects and people to some extent in my career (you have to manage people up, down, and sideways throughout a successful career), it was during this stage about three years ago that I had responsibility for ten direct reports.
> *"Not Just Another Manager" Stage:* Finally, in the fifth stage, I now differentiate myself by fostering a culture of productivity and compatibility, hiring sincere and motivated people and setting high standards that are consistently met.

It's important to note that throughout the five stages it has been personal knowledge and abilities that enabled me to be successful. At the beginning of my career, technical, industry, and job knowledge were important, but my progression is rewarded and will continue to be rewarded due to personal knowledge and organizational abilities, which are competencies honed at HBS.

What have been the obstacles and challenges of your career progression?

The biggest challenge has been managing up. I didn't realize the critical importance of managing up, especially with respect to making sure my manager understands what I'm doing. I'm not promoting brown-nosing but rather the notion of effective communication of one's ideas. What good is the world's best idea if you can't effectively communicate it? Upward management through effective communication yields believability, credibility, and promotability. It is especially important and challenging to manage up when personal rapport with the manager is not ideal. I think that talking to unbiased parties and bouncing ideas off them—mentors or peers—is a great way to assess whether you're seeing the big picture and test how such should be communicated to your superiors.

Another challenge to keep in mind is that there are advantages and disadvantages to being in your company's corporate headquarters. In fact, I think there are better reasons for *not* being at headquarters, which is contrary to what many people usually believe. People often want to be located at headquarters because they feel they will reap benefits of greater visibility to the chairman. However, so much time at headquarters is spent gossiping and not enough on business. A satellite office operates as if it were running its own business. Being in a satellite office is liberating.

The other two challenges involve people. First, don't be surprised when the seemingly most neutral colleague backstabs you. The people who openly disagree are at least willing to talk about it; however, it's the people who are quiet who are plotting their actions against you and preparing for guerrilla warfare. Never expect to win every battle. Take the long-term view. Second, career advancement requires successful people management. It requires a lot of time and attention. Don't patronize and don't ignore your people because it may come back to haunt you. People management is more time intensive and critical than technical problems. Take care of people problems first.

Can you describe an experience that has significantly influenced your career?

The experience that significantly influenced my career is when I left First Chicago to pursue a long-term management opportunity at CIBC, where I would be more than just a banker. I took a long-term perspective regarding my career and took a risk in pursuit of this long-term opportunity because I was confident in my abilities to make another move if the CIBC opportunity did not materialize. As the saying goes, "No risk, no return."

What strengths have helped you excel in your career?

Three strengths that have enabled me to excel in my career are communicating persuasively, having a long-term perspective, and completing tasks I set out to perform. With regard to the first strength, anyone can run a computer or regression analysis, but those who excel can also communicate the analysis into a coherent strategy to follow. And to the strength of always completing tasks I set out to perform, I call this "consistent integrity"— doing what I promised. I will not make commitments I cannot keep; everyone is watching everything I do.

Where do you see your career going over the next ten years? How will you prepare for such changes?

Right now I'm at a juncture. I could continue my career per the status quo, but the limiting factor is the trend of flattening organizations, and hence increasing responsibility becoming limited. I like what I do, especially with respect to managing people, and I would not mind moving into more senior management levels, which suggests that I strongly consider broadening my horizons and perspective. But doing my own thing could be fun as well. I also think about working for a client.

Preparing for the future means continuing to develop and refine my skills, talking to a lot of people, and building a network of contacts and a broad knowledge base. It would be great to have a guardian angel, but it just doesn't work that way. In fact, mentor time is limited, and career development is usually nonexistent except for the first couple of years. Advice can be expected but is often unorganized and from many sources. In short, preparing for the future is difficult.

To what extent did your HBS degree prepare you for the day-to-day life of CIBC?

HBS attracts leaders and hones those skills. Personal values, knowledge, and abilities are extremely important, and I think HBS excels at developing and refining these personal attributes. Any smart person can learn technical, industry, and job knowledge, but it's the general, broad knowledge base and personal values that enable excellence, and HBS is distinguished at developing them. Because of my HBS education, I am well organized and see the big picture. These attributes are important in the day-to-day life at CIBC. Also, HBS made me sensitive to other cultures and international differences. This is especially important in the increasingly global world and has made a significant difference in my career.

Is there anything else you would recommend to future HBS graduates entering the finance industry?

I recommend that you set short-term, mid-term, and long-term goals. Evaluate these goals for yourself and your company. Ask yourself questions and ponder answers. Are you compatible with your job and the people around you at work? Do you enjoy your job? If not, then leave, because life is too short. But to a certain extent, you also have to put up with some things you don't like.

A helpful analogy is to think of your career as an investment. You would not put money in a stock and let it sit for 50 years. You would probably look at that investment every six months. Do the same for your career; HBS is an investment in yourself. Don't keep doing something you don't like. If you're unhappy, it will be obvious in your work and in your life.

Firms Describe Themselves: Finance

During the spring of 1993, a variety of firms that typically hire MBAs for positions in finance were contacted and asked to respond to the questionnaire that appears on page 00. The firms contacted include investment banking firms, commercial banks, Fortune 500 firms, and regional companies. Responses from firms in this section are printed, for the most part, as received.

A.G. Edwards & Sons, Inc.

One North Jefferson
St. Louis, MO 63103
(314) 289-3000

MBA Recruiting Contact(s):
Primary Contact:
Lester H. Krone
(314) 289-2358
Secondary Contact:
Douglas D. Rubenstein
(314) 289-3098

Company Description

Describe your firm's business and the types of clients served by your finance group(s).

Founded in 1887, A.G. Edwards is the largest securities firm headquartered off Wall Street; it is one of the few firms described as a "national full-line" firm by the Securities and Exchange Commission and the Securities Industry Association. For over 100 years, the firm has played a major role in providing financial services to a variety of clients nationwide. From its headquarters in St. Louis, the firm and its subsidiaries provide securities and commodities brokerage, asset management, insurance, real estate, and investment banking services. Our departments provide investment banking services in the areas of Corporate Finance, Mergers and Acquisitions, and Valuations.

Public and Structured Finance, a department that is separate and distinct from those discussed below, is also part of A.G. Edwards's investment banking services. While the Public and Structured Finance department does not currently recruit on college campuses, inquiries can be made to Daniel J. Schaub, (314) 289-4343, at the address listed above.

Describe your ownership structure.

A.G. Edwards, a publicly owned corporation for over 20 years, is traded on the New York Stock Exchange under the symbol AGE.

How does your approach to finance differ from that of other firms, and what do you consider to be your strengths and distinctive capabilities?

Our success has been built in large part on our orientation toward relationship banking. Rather than emphasizing individual transactions, we provide a variety of services that meet our clients' needs and further our long-term relationships with them. Although our clients range from *Fortune* 500 corporations to small private companies, we consider our niche to be middle-market companies. We serve clients coast to coast and compete with other national, as well as regional, investment banks.

The close attention we provide clients gave A.G. Edwards the distinction of being the nation's only retail brokerage firm to be included in both editions of *The Service Edge: 101 Companies That Profit from Customer Care* and both editions of *The 100 Best Companies to Work for in America*. We attribute the firm's success to our emphasis on consistently maintaining the customers' success as a primary focus, creating value with the services we deliver and treating employees "like members of the family."

According to *Institutional Investor* at year-end 1992, A.G. Edwards was the fourth largest securities firm in the United States based on the number of offices (over 470 in 48 states), and the sixth largest based on the number of registered representatives (over 4900). Well known within the industry for our national distribution network, our distribution of securities in small amounts to a large number of investors results in a large, geographically dispersed shareholder/bondholder base for the issuer.

Discuss changes in your firm's revenues (both domestic and international) and professional staff over the past year; over the past five years.

Although most of A.G. Edwards's revenues are derived from commissions generated by selling securities to individual investors, our departments' revenues are derived from a diversified base of business that includes underwritings of equity and debt, mergers and acquisitions, valuations, and financial advisory projects. Our departments have significantly expanded both the breadth and depth of our capability over the past decade. The rapid growth of our departments affords a motivated individual the opportunity to make a meaningful contribution to A.G. Edwards. The number of professionals in the Corporate Finance, Mergers and Acquisitions, and Valuations departments has grown from 7 professionals in 1983 to over 40 professionals in 1993. All associates are hired for our St. Louis headquarters, where over 2300 of our over 10,000 employees work.

The Finance MBA's Job Description

Describe the career path and corresponding responsibilities for an MBA at your firm.

A.G. Edwards's Corporate Finance, Mergers and Acquisitions, and Valuations departments are rapidly developing areas of the company that afford talented, hardworking individuals recognition and responsibility early in their career development. A generalist program for an Associate's development is strongly emphasized, and new Associates in investment banking are given a wide variety of projects in corporate finance, mergers and acquisitions, and valuations.

A.G. Edwards emphasizes teamwork. Teams are small, and new Associates can expect to work directly on client assignments with senior investment banking professionals, ensuring the Associates' visibility and responsibility on projects. In addition, we have developed a system of semiannual and annual reviews, as well as specific project reviews, to provide individuals with feedback on their development.

Describe the opportunities for professional mobility between the various departments in your firm.

We expect Associates to be generalists in corporate finance, mergers and acquisitions, and valuations in the early stage of their careers. Because there are no rigid boundaries separating these areas, new Associates will be involved in projects in all of these areas. Associates are allowed to develop areas of expertise and specialization as they gain experience in investment banking.

Discuss the lifestyle aspects of a career with your firm (i.e., average hours per week, amount of travel, flexibility to change offices, corporate culture, etc.).

Demands and expectations at A.G. Edwards are very high. The firm, however, tries to maintain a reasonable balance between work and personal interests, which is reflected by a low turnover rate for our employees. St. Louis offers a very affordable and pleasant quality of life. The city consistently rates in the top ten of U.S. metropolitan areas in terms of quality of life. St. Louis provides an array of dance, theater, music, art, leisure activities, and sports and includes many nationally recognized landmarks. The city is also home to a significant number of *Fortune* 500 companies.

The Recruiting Process

Describe your recruiting process and the criteria by which you select candidates. Are grades a criterion? Is prior experience necessary?

Our strategy for selecting new investment banking Associates is to employ those whom we feel have the skills and compatibility to build long-term careers at A.G. Edwards. We have avoided the cutbacks common in our industry because we do not initially overhire. Instead, the number of new positions is commensurate with the firm's steady growth. Each new Associate is carefully chosen to assume a role in which long-term dedication and a commitment to manage increasing responsibility are expected.

Leadership, personal integrity, academic success, and demonstrated success in other areas are some of the criteria we use to judge individual candidates. A commitment to investment banking, shown by summer internships or relevant experience prior to graduate school, is also an important criterion.

In a typical year, how many permanent associates and analysts do you hire? Do you have a summer program for associates or analysts? If so, please describe.

We add new Associates and Analysts according to the quality of individual candidates and the compatibility of those candidates with A.G. Edwards. Therefore, we do not set yearly quotas for hiring. We have retained a very high percentage of the Associates we have hired over the past ten years.

We currently do not offer a summer program for Associates or Analysts.

What international opportunities does your firm offer for U.S. citizens? For foreign nationals?

While A.G. Edwards does participate in the international marketing of underwritings to a limited extent, all of our operations, including investment banking, are located in the United States.

Bankers Trust

280 Park Avenue 32W
New York, NY 10017
(212) 454-1767

MBA Recruiting Contact(s):
Deborah Barry
(212) 454-1767

Company Description

Describe your firm's business and the types of clients served by your finance group(s).

Bankers Trust New York Corporation, with headquarters in New York City, is a registered bank holding company incorporated in 1965. Its principal banking subsidiary, Bankers Trust Company, began business in 1903 as a trust company and became a commercial bank in 1917. In the early 1980s it sold its retail branch network and redirected its resources toward wholesale banking, focusing its businesses on major corporations, financial institutions, governments, and high net worth individuals worldwide.

Today, Bankers Trust is a universal banking company that operates in the world's financial markets to deliver tailored financial solutions to its clients and to provide superior returns to its shareholders and rewarding work to its people. All of the human and financial resources of Bankers Trust are committed to preeminence in the strategic management of risk for its clients and for the firm.

Consistent with this business strategy, the firm is organized globally into two principal units. The first, Financial Services, brings together the firm's financing, derivative, advisory, and trading capabilities. The second is Global Assets, which contains the trust, investment management, securities processing, cash management, and private banking businesses. Domestic corporate debt and equity underwriting powers are exercised by BT Securities Corporation, a wholly owned subsidiary.

Within and across these businesses there are five business functions that represent the fundamental roles that are performed in the marketplace: Client Finance, Client Advisory, Client Financial Risk Management, Client Transaction Processing, and Trading & Positioning. These functions provide diversity & stability of earnings during all phases of the market cycle.

Discuss changes in your firm's revenues (both domestic and international) and professional staff over the past year; over the past five years.

The success of Bankers Trust's business strategy has been demonstrated by its strong financial performance. Since 1979, when the strategy began to take form, net income has increased from $114 million to $761 million in 1992. Bankers Trust, with return on average common equity of 23% in 1992, is one of the most profitable major financial services companies in the world.

17

Bear Stearns & Co. Inc.

245 Park Avenue
New York, NY 10167
(212) 272-2000

MBA Recruiting Contact(s):
William E. Mills
(212) 272-3506

Company Description

Describe your firm's business and the types of clients served by your finance group(s).

The Bear Stearns Companies Inc. is the parent company for Bear Stearns & Co. Inc., a leading investment banking, securities trading, and brokerage firm with more than $3.3 billion in capital. The firm's business includes underwriting, financing activities, private placements, mergers and acquisitions, financial advisory services, real estate finance, securities research, and asset management. Through its wholly owned subsidiary, Bear Stearns Securities Corp., it provides professional and correspondent clearing services, including securities lending. Custodial Trust Company, a wholly owned subsidiary of the Bear Stearns Companies Inc., provides master trust, custody, and government clearing services.

The Bear Stearns Investment Banking Division offers a full range of financial advisory expertise in the following areas:

Corporate finance/capital markets
Financial advisory
Financial restructuring
High Yield finance
Mergers and acquisitions
Principal investments
Public finance
Structured finance

Bear Stearns offers enhanced investment banking services, including communications, emerging markets, energy, financial institutions, gaming, health care, media, retailing, technology, and utilities.

Internationally, the firm has been very active in Latin America, participating in the majority of underwritings in that region in calendar 1992. In April, the government of Pakistan selected Bear Stearns as the leader of the consortium advising it on the privatization of the Pakistan Telecommunications Corporation. There are opportunities for Associates to function in this area.

Headquartered in New York City, Bear Stearns employs more than 6200 people worldwide and maintains domestic offices in Atlanta, Boston, Chicago, Dallas, Los Angeles, and San Francisco and international offices in Frankfurt, Geneva, Hong Kong, London, Paris, and Tokyo.

The Finance MBA's Job Description

Describe the career path and corresponding responsibilities for an MBA at your firm.

Associates work on a wide variety of corporate finance and merger and acquisition transactions in numerous different industries. Often, an Associate will be working on three to five different transactions or projects at the same time, each with a different industry and transactional focus. Project teams typically consist of two to four people.

Job responsibilities include detailed financial analysis and modeling; due diligence with respect to a client's business, industry, financial results, and projects; creating new business proposals/presentations; and preparing internal memorandums for the various committees that review and approve transactions.

We look to hire individuals who have a strong accounting and finance background. Additionally, we look for candidates with work experience in credit analysis, public accounting, investment banking, as well as other related industries. We do not offer a training program.

The Recruiting Process

Describe your recruiting process and the criteria by which you select candidates. Are grades a criterion? Is prior experience necessary?

A candidate for an Associate position should exhibit the following qualifications: an outstanding academic record; involvement in extracurricular activities or outside employment; the ability to work well with others under pressure; strong oral and written communications skills; attention to detail and concern for accuracy; and a willingness to work long hours. No specific academic major is a prerequisite; however, a candidate must be comfortable with financial and mathematical concepts.

Do you have a summer program for associates or analysts? If so, please describe.

Bear Stearns has a summer Associate program in which the students are hired as generalists in investment banking and have the opportunity to work on a variety of projects in the mergers and acquisitions area, capital markets, and corporate finance. Numerous summer Associates are given full-time employment opportunities after the completion of the summer program.

BNY Associates

 small

60 State Street
Boston, MA 02109
(617) 573-9100

MBA Recruiting Contact(s):
Patricia B. Davis, Vice President

Company Description

Describe your firm's business and the types of clients served by your finance group(s).

BNY Associates is a Boston-based investment bank providing a broad range of financial advisory services to middle-market companies. The firm's transactions focus on mergers and acquisitions, private placements of debt and equity securities, restructurings, and other corporate advisory services such as fairness opinions and valuations. The staff has in aggregate over 100 years of investment banking experience. Although the firm concentrates on serving the needs of companies based in the Northeast and Mid-Atlantic regions, transactions have been completed throughout the United States in industries ranging from high technology to manufacturing and distribution, from health care to financial services.

Describe your ownership structure.

BNY Associates is a subsidiary of the Bank of New York.

How does your approach to finance differ from that of other firms, and what do you consider to be your strengths and distinctive capabilities?

We offer middle-market companies the creativity and professionalism of a highly experienced, Wall Street-trained investment banking group. We target transactions ranging from $10 million to $100 million. Because of the generalist nature of our backgrounds, we are comfortable with a wide variety of industries and have experience in almost all kinds of transactions. We feel uncomfortable with the conflicts inherent in principal activities and do not engage in any form of merchant banking. We will not engage in unfriendly takeovers but prefer to be seen as a trusted advisor to our clients.

Discuss changes in your firm's revenues (both domestic and international) and professional staff over the past year; over the past five years.

In the seven years that BNY Associates has been in existence, it has arranged over 90 transactions, completed numerous advisory assignments, and raised over $1 billion in capital for its clients.

The Finance MBA's Job Description

Describe the career path and corresponding responsibilities for an MBA at your firm.

Associates at BNY Associates work on teams composed of a Senior Investment Banker and an Analyst. The teams vary with the transactions. Associates generally work on several transactions at the same time. Because we are a small group, new Associates can expect early responsibility and meaningful involvement in a wide variety of transactions.

Describe the opportunities for professional mobility between the various departments in your firm.

New Associates work on a variety of assignments on a variety of teams across a wide spectrum of industries and transactions.

Discuss the lifestyle aspects of a career with your firm (i.e., average hours per week, amount of travel, flexibility to change offices, corporate culture, etc.).

The firm expects a great deal of hard work, sincere commitment, and significant sacrifice from all of its investment bankers. In this way, we believe our firm can excel in providing exceptional creativity and service to our clients. Nevertheless, the lifestyle permits interests outside the firm and is consistent with family responsibilities.

The Recruiting Process

Describe your recruiting process and the criteria by which you select candidates. Are grades a criterion? Is prior experience necessary?

We look for MBAs who have demonstrated potential to analyze quantitative problems quickly and effectively. Personal integrity, communications skills, leadership abilities, and academic achievements are important ingredients. We prefer candidates with two to four years of meaningful work experience.

In a typical year, how many permanent associates and analysts do you hire? Do you have a summer program for associates or analysts? If so, please describe.

BNY Associates generally hires one or two Associate(s) each year. We have not established a formal summer program for MBAs.

Bowles Hollowell Conner & Co.

227 West Trade Street
Charlotte, NC 28202
(704) 348-1000

MBA Recruiting Contact(s):
Robert G. Calton III
(704) 348-1069

Company Description

Describe your firm's business and the types of clients served by your finance group(s).

Bowles Hollowell Conner & Co. is a national investment banking firm specializing in corporate finance services for middle-market companies. From its Charlotte headquarters, the firm assists corporations, private investment firms, and middle-market companies with mergers and acquisitions; divestitures; structured financing, including private placements of senior and mezzanine debt and equity securities; and valuations. Transaction values typically range from $10 million to $150 million.

Describe your ownership structure.

Bowles Hollowell Conner & Co. is a private corporation owned by its employees.

How does your approach to finance differ from that of other firms, and what do you consider to be your strengths and distinctive capabilities?

Bowles Hollowell Conner & Co. was founded in 1975 to provide middle-market companies with a level of corporate finance expertise generally not available to them. Although the nation's largest corporations have long had the benefit of expert consultation and assistance with complex corporate finance matters, this same expertise has not been readily available to smaller companies.

The firm has been successful in helping to fill this void. A professional staff of approximately 40 employees provides clients with the high level of knowledge and experience in business, finance, accounting, law, and taxation needed for success with corporate finance transactions.

Bowles Hollowell Conner & Co. has demonstrated capability in a wide range of transactions in many different industries, from basic manufacturing to high technology and from consumer products to industrial commodities.

In all of its services, the firm emphasizes thoroughness of preparation, professionalism in execution, and effectiveness in assisting clients in meeting business objectives.

A specialty of Bowles Hollowell Conner & Co. is in the area of mergers, acquisitions, and divestitures involving companies with values less than $150 million. Clients include large corporations, private investment firms, and public and private middle-market companies. The firm represents either the buyer or the seller in a typical transaction. In addition, Bowles Hollowell Conner & Co. provides valuation services to public and private companies for purposes such as fairness opinions, employee stock ownership plans, or individual estate and gift tax purposes.

In the past several years, Bowles Hollowell Conner & Co. has increased its emphasis on assisting clients in the capital raising process and currently has four professionals devoted exclusively to this effort. The Private Financing Group is focused on raising capital for corporations for a variety of purposes, including financings, leveraged recapitalizations, and restructurings.

Discuss changes in your firm's revenues (both domestic and international) and professional staff over the past year; over the past five years.

Bowles Hollowell Conner & Co. has enjoyed tremendous growth over the last five years, and 1992 was a record year for the firm in terms of transactions completed, revenue, and profits. As such, Bowles Hollowell Conner & Co. offers a new Associate the opportunity to develop corporate finance skills in a dynamic environment.

The Finance MBA's Job Description

Describe the career path and corresponding responsibilities for an MBA at your firm.

Bowles Hollowell Conner & Co. expects each MBA whom it hires as an Associate to become a Managing Director and owner of the firm. The responsibilities of an Associate revolve around working in a team environment on a variety of transactions and generally on several transactions at the same time. As a critical member of the team, the Associate is responsible for managing the work of one or more Analysts on the team, overseeing the preparation of qualitative and quantitative analyses, ensuring the accuracy and quality of all the analytical work supporting the transaction, and relating the ideas of the firm to the client. The firm offers a flexible environment that rewards initiative and allows the Associate to develop as quickly as he or she is capable.

Describe the opportunities for professional mobility between the various departments in your firm.

Because the firm is devoted exclusively to the corporate finance needs of middle-market companies, each new professional is developed as a generalist working on a variety of assignments and teams within the firm.

Discuss the lifestyle aspects of a career with your firm (i.e., average hours per week, amount of travel, flexibility to change offices, corporate culture, etc.).

The business of the firm requires a great deal of hard work, dedication, and sacrifice. A high level of commitment is necessary to deliver financial expertise of the highest quality in the timeliest manner. Because approximately two-thirds of our assignments are outside the southeastern United States, an Associate will be required to travel regularly throughout the United States on firm business. Nevertheless, the firm respects the right of each individual to personal time away from the office, family responsibilities, and the importance of developing interests outside the firm.

In addition, involvement in outside activities within the community is viewed as an important aspect of an Associate's development, and members of the firm participate in a variety of external community activities.

The Recruiting Process

Describe your recruiting process and the criteria by which you select candidates. Are grades a criterion? Is prior experience necessary?

The firm is looking for MBAs who have demonstrated the potential to analyze financial problems quickly and effectively. We look for academic achievement, intellectual ability, demonstrated leadership abilities, personal integrity, and the ability to communicate ideas and recommendations effectively, orally as well as in writing. Although not a strict requirement, we look for individuals with two to four years of meaningful work experience.

In a typical year, how many permanent associates and analysts do you hire? Do you have a summer program for associates or analysts? If so, please describe.

Bowles Hollowell Conner & Co. expects to hire two or three Associates and five or six Analysts in the coming year. The firm has brief, formal training programs for both Associates and Analysts but strongly favors on-the-job training. Associates and Analysts are expected to become productive members of the firm quickly.

The firm currently has no summer program for MBAs, but the initiation of such a program is under consideration.

Broadview Associates, L.P.

One Bridge Plaza
Fort Lee, NJ 07024
(201) 346-9000

MBA Recruiting Contact(s):
George Carbone, Managing Associate

Company Description

Describe your firm's business and the types of clients served by your finance group(s).

Broadview Associates, L.P. is the leading merger and acquisition (M&A) firm serving companies in the global information technology (IT) industry or seeking initial participation in the industry. Founded in 1973, Broadview dominates M&A within the principal sectors of the IT industry, which encompasses software, hardware, internetworking, telecommunications, marketing/processing services, and database publishing businesses. Broadview has completed over 200 transactions in the last 5 years and over 500 in its 20-year history. In addition to M&A, Broadview services include minority investments, private placements, and strategic alliances. The firm is also a general partner in GeoCapital, a venture capital firm formed to make private equity investments in the IT industry.

Broadview represents both buyer and seller clients. Buyer clients include large IT suppliers as well as smaller, specialized IT companies. IT companies seek to secure a sustainable competitive advantage and boost shareholder value by adding technologies, products, operations, and access to markets. Frequently, their objectives can be satisfied by acquiring part or all of a niche player. On the other side, seller clients that want to manage the passage between early growth stages and sustainable, superior equity value seek to leverage the resources of a larger, more established enterprise. Typically, companies wishing to sell have developed new technologies and products, gained unique market positions, or marshaled unique human resource capabilities that they cannot fully exploit alone. An appropriate partner for a seller client can telescope market-product development cycles, provide required capital, shrink the associated risks, and gain an innovative and focused management team.

The interaction of these corporate supply and demand forces has made IT the most M&A-prone industry in the world. Given the complexity and rapid change in this industry, finding the right strategic fit can be a difficult task. As a result, buyers and sellers utilize Broadview to grasp the industry's strategic underpinnings, as well as to leverage our track record of transaction experience. Broadview has over 85 employees located in offices in Fort Lee (NJ), Redwood Shores (CA), and London (UK). Opportunities exist for career growth and development throughout the firm.

Describe your ownership structure.

Broadview Associates is structured as a limited partnership. Each of the firm's ten Managing Directors is recognized by the IT industry as an expert and spokesperson in M&A.

How does your approach to finance differ from that of other firms, and what do you consider to be your strengths and distinctive capabilities?

Developed and seasoned for 20 years, Broadview's unique set of qualifications includes the following:

- *Transaction experience.* The Managing Directors and Associates of Broadview know the IT M&A environment because of their strong roots in the IT industry. They have been founders of privately held IT companies, as well as corporate officers of public companies. Their hands-on knowledge and experience assure clients that highly informed analysis and judgment concerning the multiple aspects of an acquisition will be readily available throughout the acquisition process.

- *Concentration.* Through its experience and industry focus, Broadview offers its clients an exceptionally high degree of expertise in a dynamic and complex environment.

- *Commitment.* Broadview's deal activities mirror those of the overall IT industry. Broadview has participated in the industry's largest highly visible transactions, including the sale of Pansophic to Computer Associates and Sterling Software's merger with Systems Center. However, given that the average deal in the IT industry has a value of under $20 million, Broadview also participates in many transactions whose size is typically outside the focus of the M&A departments of traditional investment banking firms. Thus, one of Broadview's greatest strengths is its depth of experience in these middle-market transactions.

- *Contacts.* Broadview enjoys relationships with managers and directors throughout the IT industry, as well as with other players seeking to participate in this segment. In addition, Broadview maintains close working relationships with the venture capital community, given the predominance of venture-backed IT companies. This network provides unparalleled insight into the external development needs and strategies of IT companies.

- *Proprietary information.* Broadview's research department maintains the industry's most comprehensive databases in support of the firm's M&A and minority investment activity. The firm maintains active files on over 30,000 companies, as well as a proprietary database of IT industry acquisitions. Since 1980, in partnership with the Information Technology Association of America (formerly ADAPSO), Broadview has published the semiannual *Broadview Merger Report*, which tracks and analyzes M&A activity and valuation benchmarks within the industry. This report is well recognized throughout the industry and serves as a valuable tool for both marketing to prospective clients and valuing companies engaged in transactions.

The Finance MBA's Job Description

Describe the career path and corresponding responsibilities for an MBA at your firm.

Associates are quickly given client management responsibility. The Associate assists in the development of acquisition and divestiture strategies, identifies companies in relevant IT segments that represent potential partners, handles approaches to target companies, and ultimately helps to structure and negotiate deals between client and target companies. In managing the client relationship, the Associate usually serves as part of a three-person team, joined by a Managing Director and an Analyst. Each team member has unique responsibility and interacts daily. The Associate manages daily client contact and assists in coordinating activities among the team members.

Discuss the lifestyle aspects of a career with your firm (i.e., average hours per week, amount of travel, flexibility to change offices, corporate culture, etc.).

Broadview attracts and seeks dedicated, self-motivated professionals who can generate a superior quality of work without sacrificing their lifestyles. Travel is required, but the extent varies by specific assignment.

The Recruiting Process

Describe your recruiting process and the criteria by which you select candidates. Are grades a criterion? Is prior experience necessary?

Broadview seeks individuals with excellent written and oral communication skills, transaction experience, and demonstrated interest or experience in the IT industry. The ideal candidate must also be a highly motivated self-starter and possess interpersonal skills.

Do you have a summer program for associates or analysts? If so, please describe.

The firm does not have an Associate summer program.

What international opportunities does your firm offer for U.S. citizens? For foreign nationals?

Broadview's London office is staffed by U.S. citizens and foreign nationals from France, Germany, the U.K., and other European countries. Candidates for the London office typically have foreign language fluency.

Brown Brothers Harriman & Co.

59 Wall Street
New York, NY 10005
(212) 483-1818

MBA Recruiting Contact(s):
Allan B. Wechsler, Personnel Manager

Company Description

Describe your firm's business and the types of clients served by your finance group(s).

Brown Brothers Harriman & Co. is the oldest and largest private bank in the United States and the only commercial bank with a direct membership on the New York Stock Exchange and other principal U.S. exchanges. In executing transactions of corporate securities, however, the firm acts only as agent for its clients and does not participate in underwritings nor make markets in a dealer capacity.

Brown Brothers Harriman has the unique ability to offer clients a truly comprehensive financial service, including investment management, brokerage, custody of securities, and banking. Banking services include deposit accounts, commercial loans, letters of credit, foreign exchange, and corporate finance. As a bank of deposit, Brown Brothers Harriman & Co. is supervised by the banking authorities in New York, Massachusetts, and Pennsylvania. In addition, the Brown Brothers Harriman Trust Companies provide fiduciary services to complement both the investment and banking functions.

The firm's 33 General Partners and over 450 professionals operate from nine domestic and seven international offices. Brown Brothers Harriman & Co. has over $100 million in equity capital and more than $1 billion in assets. The firm holds over $100 billion of securities in custody for banks, mutual funds, and other financial institutions from around the world.

Describe your ownership structure.

Brown Brothers Harriman & Co. is a private commercial bank established as a partnership in 1818. The partners own and manage the firm and play an active role in all client relationships.

The Finance MBA's Job Description

Describe the career path and corresponding responsibilities for an MBA at your firm.

Brown Brothers Harriman & Co. provides challenges for MBAs in four areas: commercial banking, investment management, international sales, and corporate finance.

Commercial Bankers work with a select group of clients with special banking needs. Their support and advice will have a major impact on a client's success.

Investment Specialists move into portfolio management following completion of our five-month Officer Training Program. Other possibilities include institutional sales or equity research.

Account Managers in our International Institutional Sales Group, a major growth area, provide advisory services to our overseas clients, with an emphasis on U.S. equities. Candidates should be eager to work in London, Paris, Zurich, Hong Kong, or Tokyo. They should also have the appropriate language skills and meet residency requirements.

Account Managers in International Private Banking will market the firm's banking and investment services to sophisticated investors in Europe, Latin America, and the Far East from a home base in New York.

Corporate Finance Associates are given as much responsibility and freedom of action as they are willing and able to accept. While not required to specialize by industry, they are encouraged to develop expertise in areas of special interest.

Except for Corporate Finance Associates, MBAs spend their first five months in our Officer Training Program, which has a strong international focus and forges close relationships among the bank's future leaders. In their regular assignments, MBAs work with Partners and Senior Managers in a collegial environment that stresses the highest standards of professionalism, service, and integrity.

The Recruiting Process

Describe your recruiting process and the criteria by which you select candidates. Are grades a criterion? Is prior experience necessary?

We look for bright, creative people who are interested in seriously pursuing a career in the financial services industry. Successful candidates need an ability to work closely with others, solve problems, and generate new ideas. Foreign language skills and relevant work experience are pluses; superior academic achievement is a must.

In a typical year, how many permanent associates and analysts do you hire? Do you have a summer program for associates or analysts? If so, please describe.

Each year we hire 10–12 candidates.

Burns Fry Limited

1 First Canadian Place
Suite 5000
P.O. Box 150
Toronto, Ontario M5X 1H3
Canada
(416) 359-4000

MBA Recruiting Contact(s):
Mike Armstrong, Director

Company Description

Describe your firm's business and the types of clients served by your finance group(s).

One of the leading fully integrated investment dealers in Canada, Burns Fry was created in 1976 through the merger of Burns Bros. and Denton, a firm with strong equity trading and underwriting capabilities, and Fry Mills Spence, a firm with a strong debt trading and underwriting orientation. The combined strengths of these two firms, which had been conducting successful securities businesses since 1932 and 1925, respectively, resulted in a complementary blend of skills and experience, a large capital base, and a strong branch office system.

Burns Fry is now one of the largest Canadian investment dealers, in terms of both capital employed and distribution capabilities. Over 1700 employees provide services in 32 offices in Canada and in 9 international offices in the United States, Europe, and the Far East.

In order to increase our presence in the global finance community and provide greater opportunities and benefits for our clients, Burns Fry developed a networking relationship with Hoare Govett (United Kingdom and Asia), McIntosh Hamson (Australia), and Hendry Hay (New Zealand).

Our people, our capital, and our network of offices have been molded into what we believe to be the most balanced of the fully diversified securities dealers in Canada, providing our clients with state-of-the-art advice and analysis to solve financial problems and identify market opportunities.

We provide the following range of services:

- *Corporate finance.* As manager or co-manager, Burns Fry captured over 70% of all dealer-managed corporate underwritings in Canada in our fiscal year ended September 1992. We were ranked second in total corporate issues for 1991 in a recent *Financial Post* survey.

1. *Mergers, acquisitions, and divestitures.* We have the largest professional group of any other Canadian investment dealer devoted to M&A and have completed over 200 transactions for corporate and government clients representing more than $50 billion in value over the past five years.

2. *Economic and investment research.* Burns Fry provides a breadth and quality of knowledge that has brought us our number 1 ranking in independent surveys of Canadian institutional investors for the past six years.

3. *Institutional equity sales and trading.* Burns Fry handled approximately 11% of the total value of Canadian equities traded in 1992, once again making the firm the premier trader of Canadian equities worldwide.

4. *Fixed income sales and trading.* Burns Fry is one of the top-tier distributors and traders of Canadian government and corporate debt securities in the world. During 1992 we increased our trading and sales staff, expanded the range of products offered, and expanded our fixed income research and liability management group.

5. *Financial futures and options.* Through our association with international futures and options firms, we provide an international network of specialists with around-the-world 24-hour service on all major exchanges.

6. *Investor services.* Burns Fry has over 460 investment executives at 32 branches providing quality investment products and services to individual investing clients.

7. *Investment management.* Burns Fry designs and manages investment portfolios for high-net-worth individuals, pension funds, estates, and foundations and offers mutual funds through Jones Heward Investment Management Limited.

8. *Government services.* Burns Fry's Government Services Group provides financial advisory and underwriting services to federal, provincial, territorial, and municipal governments, agencies, and Crown corporations.

Describe your ownership structure.

Burns Fry is the only major Canadian investment banking and securities firm that is controlled by its employees and thereby is truly independent. Our employee shareholders own a 70% equity interest and a 90.1% voting interest in the firm; the remaining interest is held by BankAmerica Corporation, one of America's largest banks.

How does your approach to finance differ from that of other firms, and what do you consider to be your strengths and distinctive capabilities?

We believe that what differentiates Burns Fry from other investment dealers is our dedication to being the best at what we do rather than the biggest. This focus on uncompromising quality and integrity is incorporated in all aspects of the way we do business. It underpins the success we have had in identifying financing opportunities and designing new products, the preeminence we have achieved as a major market maker in Canadian corporate and government securities, and the stature we have attained as a world-ranked mergers and acquisitions financial advisor. Our work throughout has been supported by our top-ranked economics and investment research team.

Our Investment Banking department provides expertise in all areas of investment banking, including corporate finance, mergers, acquisitions and divestitures, restructuring, consulting, and financial advisory services. We achieve success for our clients by having a thorough understanding of client needs combined with a sensitivity and swift response to market opportunities. For Burns Fry, a corporate client relationship is a long-term partnership. Conscious of our continuing obligation to provide financial service, a team of highly skilled individuals is assembled to ensure full client coverage. Our team approach to assignments serves as a catalyst to combine experience and knowledge with innovation and creativity.

Investment Banking includes industry specialists who focus on the real estate, mining, financial services, forest products, communications, utilities, oil and gas, and consumer products industries. Industry specialists work closely with product specialists. The approach of our Investment Banking Group is to combine an in-depth knowledge of our clients' needs and goals with creative thought, a thorough understanding of the capital markets, and integrity.

Discuss changes in your firm's revenues (both domestic and international) and professional staff over the past year; over the past five years.

Burns Fry has consistently improved its ranking in the Canadian securities league tables over the past five years and has maintained its position as the largest trader of Canadian equities worldwide.

The Finance MBA's Job Description

Describe the career path and corresponding responsibilities for an MBA at your firm.

Career opportunities are available in all areas of the firm, including Fixed Income and Equity Sales and Trading, Liability Management, Research, Economics, Portfolio Management, and Investment Banking.

Burns Fry encourages Investment Banking Associates to generalize during the first year or two in order to develop a broad range of investment banking skills. First-year assignments may include working on a variety of corporate financing and M&A-related projects, including prospectus or offering memorandum work, analysis of a corporation's financing needs, drafting corporate presentations, assisting on valuations and fairness opinions, managing solicitations, and assisting in the marketing of new issues, both private and public. Following exposure to a wide variety of transactions, Associates may wish to specialize in a particular industry or product group. Investment Banking specialty groups and functions include underwriting, M&A, real estate, mining, communications, special products, capital markets, and consulting and advisory services.

Describe the opportunities for professional mobility between the various departments in your firm.

Opportunities for interdepartmental exchanges are offered as part of the development of professionals in our firm.

Discuss the lifestyle aspects of a career with your firm (i.e., average hours per week, amount of travel, flexibility to change offices, corporate culture, etc.).

Burns Fry is the only investment bank ranked as one of the *Financial Post*'s 100 best companies to work for in Canada. It offers a dynamic, challenging work environment with tremendous career opportunities. Burns Fry stresses a team-oriented approach to assignments and encourages an environment open to providing innovative solutions for clients.

The commitment required to provide the quality of work required in the competitive investment banking environment is considerable, particularly for new recruits. Lifestyles vary according to department.

The Recruiting Process

Describe your recruiting process and the criteria by which you select candidates. Are grades a criterion? Is prior experience necessary?

We look for highly motivated individuals with strong analytical skills, sound judgment, and a high level of integrity. Academic achievement is important. Prior related work experience is an asset.

In a typical year, how many permanent associates and analysts do you hire? Do you have a summer program for associates or analysts? If so, please describe.

In a typical year, Burns Fry hires two or three Associates, two or three Research Analysts, and others as required. We have hired summer analysts in conjunction with certain educational institutions.

Chevron Corporation

225 Bush Street
San Francisco, CA 94104-4289
(415) 894-2752

MBA Recruiting Contact(s):
Craig S. Isom, Supervisor
Finance MBA Development Program

Company Description

Describe your firm's business and the types of clients served by your finance group(s).

Chevron Corporation is an international, integrated petroleum company consistently ranked among the leaders of the *Fortune* 500. Approximately 50,000 employees generate $40 billion in annual revenues and are responsible for nearly $35 billion in assets.

Headquartered in San Francisco, we are the largest producer of petroleum products and natural gas in the United States. Chevron has operations in over 100 countries and is pursuing worldwide ventures in petroleum exploration, production, refining, and marketing. Chevron is an industry leader that is positioned for international growth, building on a rich history of innovation and making the investments needed to provide the world with clean, safe, and economical energy.

In an age of accelerating globalization of the world's national economies, the petroleum industry was one of the first and remains one of the largest, truly global enterprises. The products of this industry can truly be said to drive the engine of our global economy, providing the energy to run our factories, fuel our transportation networks, and heat our homes. This industry vividly defines the risk/reward trade-off: only one multi million-dollar well drilled out of nine has historically resulted in a commercially viable find, and capital-intensive developments often require investments of billions of dollars over time horizons of 10–50 years.

The Finance MBA's Job Description

Describe the career path and corresponding responsibilities for an MBA at your firm.

We are always seeking highly motivated individuals to help us achieve our goals. Chevron recruits MBAs to bring bright, highly skilled, and ambitious individuals with leadership and management potential into the finance function. Our goal is to develop senior financial management, including such positions as Vice President of Finance, Comptroller, and Treasurer, both at the corporate level and at any of our worldwide operating companies (predominantly headquartered in the Bay Area). Chevron pursues a deliberate policy to give top performers experience in many financial arenas in preparation for senior management.

In order to launch MBAs into this environment, Chevron maintains the Finance MBA Development Program, designed to give MBAs rapid exposure to the company and the finance function. This is a select, entry-level program that has been successfully developing financial and general managers for nearly 50 years. The program provides its members with four six-month assignments over a two-year period and is designed to give them broad exposure to financial and operating activities throughout the corporation. In addition, it provides MBAs with opportunities to apply the financial skills they acquired in business school to activities that contribute directly to the achievement of Chevron's business goals. These assignments are generally equal in responsibility to entry-level positions offered to graduating MBAs by other companies.

The assignments available to program members are located typically in organizations where financial skills are at a premium—corporate units such as the Comptroller's and Treasurer's departments, plus finance, planning, and other functional positions at major operating companies such as Chevron U.S.A. Production, Chevron U.S.A. Products, Chevron Chemical, Chevron Shipping, and Chevron International Oil. There is no preestablished sequence of assignments. Instead, a balanced program is tailored to fit each individual's evolving needs and preferences while meeting the company's changing business requirements.

Having rapidly acquired expertise in many of Chevron's business areas and a wide range of company contacts, program members are placed in challenging positions at the program's conclusion. Many MBAs return to a group in which they had program assignments, while others undertake positions in areas new to them. An individual's personal preferences are considered in conjunction with company needs. By virtue of the high caliber of the participants and the broad experience they have gained in the program, MBAs are in great demand and are well positioned to pursue careers leading to senior financial and, often, general managerial positions.

The Recruiting Process

Describe your recruiting process and the criteria by which you select candidates. Are grades a criterion? Is prior experience necessary?

Applicants must have authorization to work on a full-time basis in the United States (does not include practical training authorization). Although Chevron does not restrict candidates to specific majors or levels of work experience, the Finance MBA Development Program is considered to be most attractive to MBAs with a strong interest in finance who welcome the opportunity to gain rapid exposure to a wide variety of financial activities at Chevron. On average, program members have two to four years of work experience before obtaining their MBA.

In a typical year, how many permanent associates and analysts do you hire? Do you have a summer program for associates or analysts? If so, please describe.

We hire just five to ten MBAs into the Finance MBA Development Program each year.

The Finance MBA Development Program sponsors an ongoing summer internship program. Similar to full-time Development Program members, summer interns are challenged by hands-on, meaningful work that provides an opportunity to experience the issues and actions of one of the world's leading corporations. Interns are placed within corporate groups (Treasury, Comptroller's, Planning) and operating companies (e.g., Chevron U.S.A. Products, Shipping, Chemical).

Internships are typically project oriented, utilizing strong analytical, organizational, and communication skills. Application of financial theory to actual business problem solving is encouraged. All positions are in the San Francisco Bay Area. Exposure to the company and managers outside each intern's particular work group is enhanced by a series of communications meetings, organizational presentations, and other activities. Interns usually have the opportunity to present their accomplishments and conclusions to finance managers at the end of the summer.

In recruiting summer interns, we look for individuals with strong interpersonal and analytical skills, leadership potential, and knowledge of a broad range of financial theory, from financial accounting to capital markets. Prospective interns should have long-term interests in careers in financial management. Again, applicants must have authorization to work on a full-time basis in the United States (does not include practical training authorization).

What international opportunities does your firm offer for U.S. citizens? For foreign nationals?

Although the domestic petroleum industry can certainly be characterized as mature, Chevron continues to pursue growth opportunities around the globe. We recently signed a joint venture petroleum production agreement with Kazakhstan that represents the largest commercial partnership between the West and what was formerly a republic of the Soviet Union.

MBAs can almost immediately gain exposure to our international operations with Bay Area assignments working in the worldwide headquarters of our international subsidiaries. Limited opportunities to work overseas are generally not available to our new hires until they have gained a minimum of three to five years' domestic experience, largely a reflection of the complexities and scope of our business. We historically have not hired foreign national MBAs into our Development Program.

D.H. Blair Investment Banking Corp.

44 Wall Street
New York, NY 10005
(212) 495-4000

MBA Recruiting Contact(s):
J. Morton Davis, Chairman
(212) 495-4500

Company Description

Describe your firm's business and the types of clients served by your finance group(s).

D.H. Blair is an independent investment bank based in New York City. The firm has a capital base of over $200 million. Blair specializes in financings of small and medium-size growth companies, as well as early-stage venture financings. Established in 1904, D.H. Blair has a strong and growing track record of providing financing for these types of companies. Equity financings include initial public offerings, private placements, venture capital, merchant banking, and mergers and acquisitions. Leveraged buyout (LBO) debt financings are growing in number and size at Blair. As a result of our long-standing relationships built up over many years with these companies, Blair has the opportunity to provide many investment banking services to its clients.

Describe your ownership structure.

D.H. Blair is an independent, privately held investment bank.

How does your approach to finance differ from that of other firms, and what do you consider to be your strengths and distinctive capabilities?

D.H. Blair is a focused, well-capitalized investment bank. It does not attempt to provide services outside its specific niche. The firm provides private and public equity and debt financing for small- and medium-size emerging-growth and high-technology companies. D.H. Blair has purposely remained an agile, niche organization with a strong capital base and retail client base. This gives us the flexibility and strength to act very quickly on finding and funding significant investment opportunities. Due to the numerous client and portfolio companies served over many years, D.H. Blair has developed relationships with several of the largest industrial and service companies in the United States as well as overseas. These relationships have led to many acquisitions, joint ventures, and other forms of investment in these D.H. Blair companies.

Discuss changes in your firm's revenues (both domestic and international) and professional staff over the past year; over the past five years.

D.H. Blair is located in New York City. The Investment Banking Group includes approximately 30 individuals. The firm has grown rapidly over the past decade and is committed to maintaining this growth. Because D.H. Blair is an entrepreneurial firm serving this nation's entrepreneurs, the current national trend toward increased levels of this activity provides even greater demands for our services.

The Finance MBA's Job Description

Describe the career path and corresponding responsibilities for an MBA at your firm.

The Corporate Finance Department of D.H. Blair considers highly motivated and aggressive MBAs who have a great deal of initiative and desire to work in various areas of investment banking. Public and private placements of equity and debt securities, as well as merchant banking, venture capital, and LBOs, are areas of opportunity at D.H. Blair. Due to the firm's entrepreneurial flair and structure, there is a great deal of opportunity for the aggressive individual to assume primary responsibility at an early stage. Thinly staffed teams allow us to recruit people looking to take on responsibility quickly. The investment banker should be able to handle all aspects of a deal, as opposed to being a transaction specialist. The banker should be able to understand all areas of a client's business, including knowledge of product, market, financial, and other nonfinancial analyses. The banker should be able to assist in management presentation, negotiation, and sales. Also, the investment banker will be responsible for solicitation of new business opportunities. The speed at which the banker will grow in importance at the firm will depend on the banker's ability to assume responsibility and develop business opportunities.

Describe the opportunities for professional mobility between the various departments in your firm.

Career paths vary greatly depending on an individual's abilities and goals. There is not the rigid structure found in larger investment banks. D.H. Blair encourages individuals to experiment in new areas in order to seek out the best opportunities and further their career goals. Due to the thin staffing structure, there is plenty of opportunity for the banker to be observed by and interact with the staff in order to determine which areas are the most appropriate for career growth.

Discuss the lifestyle aspects of a career with your firm (i.e., average hours per week, amount of travel, flexibility to change offices, corporate culture, etc.).

A career at D.H. Blair is challenging and requires dedication, hard work, and flexibility. Lifestyles vary depending on the individual's own goals as well as those of the group in which the banker works.

The Recruiting Process

Describe your recruiting process and the criteria by which you select candidates. Are grades a criterion? Is prior experience necessary?

We seek people with a history of achievement and success. These candidates show a great deal of initiative and aggressiveness, as well as the requisite analytical skills and strong interpersonal skills. Many successful candidates have had previous work experience, although it is not required. Although grades are a meaningful criterion, each candidate is considered as a combination of many abilities, and no single one is dominant.

In a typical year, how many permanent associates and analysts do you hire? Do you have a summer program for associates or analysts? If so, please describe.

D.H. Blair hires between two and four associates each year. Although D.H. Blair offers no formal training, there is very thorough on-the-job training.

D.H. Blair has no formal summer program. We hire Summer Associates, depending on availability and need, in investment banking and brokerage.

Donaldson, Lufkin & Jenrette

140 Broadway
New York, NY 10005
(212) 504-3000

MBA Recruiting Contact(s):
Andrea B. Byrnes, Vice President
(212) 504-3903

Company Description

Describe your firm's business and the types of clients served by your finance group(s).

Donaldson, Lufkin & Jenrette (DLJ) is a top-ranked, full-service investment and merchant bank. Founded in 1959 by three entrepreneurial Harvard MBAs as a research boutique specializing in institutional equity analysis, DLJ has developed premier franchises in the research, sales, trading, and underwriting of equity and fixed income securities. These franchises extend to all major sectors of the capital markets and complement the firm's expertise in mergers and acquisitions and merchant banking. In 1985, DLJ merged with the Equitable Life Assurance Society of the United States.

As a flexible, midsize firm, DLJ seized the growth opportunities presented by the turbulent markets of 1989–1990 to add high-caliber professionals to its staff and to expand into new market segments. In 1992 DLJ was the top-ranked underwriter of issues rated single-B or lower, has achieved significant gains in the investment-grade corporate bond sector (which had been targeted for growth), and has become a power in the mortgage-backed securities market. DLJ has successfully grown its businesses by focusing on transactions in which the quality of ideas and execution skills can make a difference in clients' performance.

How does your approach to finance differ from that of other firms, and what do you consider to be your strengths and distinctive capabilities?

Time and again this year, DLJ's approach to capital raising, merchant banking, and venture capital investing yielded superior results for our clients and portfolio companies. We believe that no transaction is easy or routine; each requires the personal attention and commitment of senior professionals. We have gathered a comparatively small group of superior bankers, and we encourage them to commit DLJ's capital and diverse talents to transac-

tions of the highest quality. The current wave of consolidation in the securities industry will place a premium on this approach, which values close client relationships and innovative solutions leveraged by intelligent use of capital and strong institutional distribution capabilities.

Discuss changes in your firm's revenues (both domestic and international) and professional staff over the past year; over the past five years.

By any measure, 1992 was an extraordinary year for the securities industry and, unquestionably, the most significant and successful in DLJ's 33-year history. On the heels of 1991's record revenues and earnings, DLJ reached a level of profitability in 1992 that we had expected to achieve only after three or four more years of solid growth. The most encouraging aspect of this exceptional performance was that it validated, in the strongest possible manner, the strategy that has been guiding DLJ's development over the past six years.

The Finance MBA's Job Description

Describe the career path and corresponding responsibilities for an MBA at your firm.

Investment Banking
Associates in the Investment Banking Division work in small project teams of a Managing Director or Senior Vice President, a Vice President, and an Analyst. An Associate may work on four or five assignments simultaneously, ranging from mergers and divestitures to private placements or public offerings. By the end of the first year, Associates are expected to assume a high degree of responsibility for both project management and client maintenance.

Public Finance
Associates initially rotate through product groups within the division and are then placed in a group depending on where the Associates are needed and on individual interest. During the first year, an Associate is exposed to all aspects of a transaction, from getting the business to selling and closing a bond issue. Working closely with senior bankers on each project, the Associate will write proposals and organize presentations. As the Public Finance Associate develops, he or she will become more involved in various phases of client contact and presentations.

Institutional Equity Research
The entry-level Analyst is given immediate responsibility for coverage of an industry that will be mutually agreed upon. The position entails development of specialized

analytical skills, frequent interviews with senior corporate managers, company visits, secondary research, and ultimately intensive interpersonal marketing. A group of senior Analysts will be fully accessible to, and will assist in the development of, the new Analyst. Ultimately it is the individual's responsibility to build a franchise of authority and expertise within the investment community through his or her written product and client interaction.

Institutional Equity Sales

Sales professionals are responsible for transmitting research recommendations generated by Analysts and banking products generated by the Investment Banking Division to analysts and portfolio managers at institutional firms. Sales Associates will spend the first six months in a formal Equities Division training program that incorporates rotation on various desks; daily meetings with Research Analysts; a research department project; tri-weekly meetings with senior sales professionals, including role-playing sessions; and a two- to three-day regional office rotation. Following training, a new Associate takes on direct account responsibility.

Taxable Fixed Income

The Taxable Fixed Income Division recruits MBAs for its sales, trading, and research areas. In the sales and trading areas, new MBAs are assigned to work closely with experienced professionals for the first six months to learn the ropes.

Describe the opportunities for professional mobility between the various departments in your firm.

DLJ hires Associates directly into the various departments described above. There is no preplanned mobility among departments, but if interest is expressed and the individual has demonstrated competence, there is some opportunity to move to a different area of specialization. An Associate who joined DLJ's Investment Banking Division in 1982 now heads the High Yield Department in the Taxable Fixed Income Division, and a professional formerly in our Public Finance Division is now in corporate finance.

Discuss the lifestyle aspects of a career with your firm (i.e., average hours per week, amount of travel, flexibility to change offices, corporate culture, etc.).

The lifestyle aspects of a career with DLJ vary from department to department. Nevertheless, some career choices place large demands on an individual's time. DLJ's corporate culture emphasizes excellence, informality, and independent initiative. We want our Associates to take pride in personal and corporate accomplishments, assuming early responsibility without losing sight of our traditional final corporate objective: to have fun!

The Recruiting Process

Describe your recruiting process and the criteria by which you select candidates. Are grades a criterion? Is prior experience necessary?

New MBAs are hired principally into the Investment Banking Division, with additional opportunities in Equity and Fixed Income Research, Equity and Fixed Income Sales and Trading, and Public Finance. Associates are hired as generalists, providing them with the flexibility to explore a broad array of financial instruments and client transactions. A decentralized, results-oriented management style creates an entrepreneurial atmosphere and encourages initiative through goal-oriented compensation.

DLJ has no predetermined criteria in evaluating potential Associates. Prior experience in finance, while helpful, is not required. More important, we look for individuals whose work experience emphasizes initiative, excellence, and creativity.

In a typical year, how many permanent associates and analysts do you hire? Do you have a summer program for associates or analysts? If so, please describe.

In a typical year, the Investment Banking Division hires 15–20 Associates and 25–30 Analysts. We conduct two separate orientation programs in the fall, but most of the training will be on-the-job experience.

We hire 12–15 summer Associates and 10–12 summer Analysts.

Enron Gas Services Corporation

1400 Smith Street
Houston, TX 77002
(713) 853-6614

MBA Recruiting Contact(s):
Lucy Marshall
MBA Recruiting Coordinator

Company Description

Describe your firm's business and the types of clients served by your finance group(s).

Enron Gas Services (EGS), the merchant arm of the $6 billion Enron Corp., was formed approximately three years ago to compete in the rapidly changing natural gas industry. An innovative business strategy and aggressive style has earned EGS a proud reputation within a short period of time. We are the largest buyer and seller of natural gas in North America and one of the largest traders of natural gas on the NYMEX and in the over-the-counter energy commodity derivatives market. An overriding objective of EGS is to become the most innovative and reliable provider of clean energy worldwide for a better environment, today and tomorrow.

Since its deregulation, the natural gas industry has experienced extreme price volatility—the highest for any other commodity in the world. EGS is the leader and innovator in providing stability to the industry by offering a variety of long-term known-price gas contracts and low-cost funding mechanisms to producers and end users. During 1992, EGS solidified its position as the largest nonregulated gas merchant in North America, ranked at or near the top in a number of categories:

- Manager of the largest portfolio of fixed-price and natural gas derivative contracts in the world.

- Among the leading entities arranging for new capital to the independent oil and gas industry in the United States.

- Operator of the largest pipeline system in Texas, Houston Pipe Line (HPL).

- Operator of a major pipeline in Louisiana, Louisiana Resources Company (LRC), that interconnects to most major interstate pipelines in the Northeast, Southeast, and Midwest.

- Largest supplier of gas to the electric generation industry in North America.

- One of the largest marketers and merchants of natural gas liquids in the United States.

Through an aggressive customer segmentation strategy, EGS serves almost every commercial market in the industry with customized physical and financial natural gas products. EGS activities can be grouped into three primary business areas:

1. Supply origination groups secure natural gas supplies and related products from independent producers through a variety of financial techniques, including long-term contracting, acquisition financing, and price hedging.

2. Market origination groups sell gas products to a broad range of consumers, such as local distribution companies, cogeneration facilities, electric utilities, and large industrials.

3. Logistics and price management groups manage the physical and financial risk incurred by EGS through its merchant activities to ensure reliable delivery at predictable prices to a rapidly changing industry.

How does your approach to finance differ from that of other firms, and what do you consider to be your strengths and distinctive capabilities?

EGS is a leader in the natural gas industry in developing innovative physical and financial products for independent producers and end users. There are two specific groups within EGS that rely heavily on finance skills and abilities.

Enron Finance Corp (EFC) arranges for funding of reserves that provide EGS with long-term supply commitments. EFC has developed unique programs to provide acquisition capital and price hedging to independent producers. One product offered by EFC is the volumetric production payment (VPP). With the VPP, EFC receives a stated volume of the producer's oil and gas production over time. The producer, in exchange, receives cash up front as a purchase price for the production. With more than $800 million in production payments originated as of June 1993, EFC has solidified its position as one of the largest entities arranging for capital to the independent oil and gas sector in North America. The debt and equity raised to fund these products does not affect Enron's balance sheet. EFC forms special companies designed to fund asset acquisitions. Through these companies, EFC packages collateralized natural gas reserves and sells them to banks and institutional investors, much like a bank packages homes loans and resells them. EFC has recently begun targeting the consumption side of the market by designing funding mechanisms specifically tailored to the capital needs of end users.

Enron Risk Management Services (ERMS) provides structured risk management products that are physical and/or financial in nature to producers, consumers, investors, and lenders in the energy industry. ERMS acts as principal in a wide variety of structured product transactions, such as swaps, caps, floors, collars, swaptions, participating swaps, product spreads, and product spread options. These products are an integral part of the long-term contracts offered in the supply and market origination groups. Recently *Risk Magazine*, a leading trade publication, ranked ERMS first among commodity traders in natural gas short-term swaps, long-term swaps, and exotic products and structured transactions, and second in options trading. ERMS is also active in the exchange of physicals (EFP) market, trading roughly 25% of the monthly EFP volume on the NYMEX.

The Recruiting Process

Describe your recruiting process and the criteria by which you select candidates. Are grades a criterion? Is prior experience necessary?

EGS is seeking candidates for its Associate program who have received an MBA degree and have at least two years of work experience. EGS generally hires 10–15 Associates a year. The Associate program operates on a rotational basis. Associates spend from one to two years providing commercial and analytical support to a variety of EGS profit centers on three- to six-month rotations and then move into commercial positions within these profit centers. The program is designed to give new hires exposure to all facets of EGS's approach to marketing physical and financial natural gas products before giving them commercial responsibilities. This gives our commercial groups a pool of talent unparalleled in the gas industry.

Candidates are not required to have a natural gas background, although prior knowledge or work experience in the energy industry is helpful. More important, EGS is looking for bright, highly motivated individuals interested in applying their skills in a fast-paced and dynamic work environment. EGS's transactions demand a high level of industry analysis, quantitative and interpersonal expertise, and self-motivation. Transactions and projects include reserve acquisitions, asset securitization, trading and risk management, and structuring and negotiation of the purchase and sale of large gas packages. Execution of these transactions requires extensive client contact and interaction with EGS management.

As the most innovative company in the natural gas industry, EGS recognizes the importance of rewarding outstanding Associates through career advancement and performance-based compensation.

FMC Corporation

200 East Randolph Drive
Chicago, IL 60601
Phone (312) 861-6000
Fax: (312) 861-5902

MBA Recruiting Contact(s):
FMC College Relations
Phone (312) 861-6000
Fax: (312) 861-5902

Company Description

Describe your firm's business and the types of clients served by your finance group(s).

FMC is a New York Stock Exchange–listed, $4 billion, Chicago-based multinational corporation producing machinery and chemicals for industry, agriculture, and government. Our worldwide work force of 22,000 staffs 95 manufacturing facilities and mines in 18 countries.

Our competitive edge in manufacturing excellence, technological innovation, cost control, and customer satisfaction has made us a leader in the global markets we serve. Earning a consistently high real return on shareholder equity is a challenge and an imperative. At FMC, the finance function is committed to increasing value today while positioning the company for future profitable growth and strategic development.

FMC is a corporate leader in developing and implementing state-of-the-art analytical techniques for financial planning, performance measurement, and resource allocation. For example, FMC recapitalized in 1986, doubling shareholder value, while enabling FMC to continue its vigorous program of internal development, capital investment, and research and development. We have also adopted an innovative current cost accounting system to assist top management in evaluating performance and strategic investment decision making. At one of our plants, we are implementing a new activity-based costing, which will give our management a deeper understanding of our product costs.

This philosophy of financial innovation pervades the entire corporation. Financial managers are active leaders of the management team and are required to think and act strategically. They are involved in all facets of managing FMC's complex businesses, from product planning to international investment decisions. Therefore, we seek highly motivated individuals who will become both our future financial leaders and future general managers.

The Finance MBA's Job Description

Describe the career path and corresponding responsibilities for an MBA at your firm.

Financial Business Analysts begin their careers in the Chicago Corporate Operations Analysis Department, where they are responsible for analyzing, monitoring, and tracking the performance of specific business segments. Analysts also work with line management on a variety of projects that affect management decisions and business performance. After 9–15 months, most Analysts assume positions in financial management in one of our line organizations. It is also possible for Analysts to pursue other functions at this point. Their choices often depend on their career focus: specializing in a functional discipline or taking advantage of FMC's opportunities for cross-functional career growth. In addition, Financial Business Analysts are in demand for a wide variety of offshore opportunities.

The Recruiting Process

In a typical year, how many permanent associates and analysts do you hire? Do you have a summer program for associates or analysts? If so, please describe.

FMC recruits at six to eight major business schools. Typically, we hire 15–25 full-time MBAs and 12–20 interns each year in the Planning, Manufacturing, Human Resources, and Finance functions.

The First Boston Corporation

Park Avenue Plaza
New York, NY 10055
(212) 909-2000

MBA Recruiting Contact(s):
Maryann K. Noonan
MBA Recruiting—Investment Banking
(212) 909-2482

Gail S. Kamhi, Vice President—Sales and Trading
(212) 909-2208

Victoria A. Longo, Vice President—Public Finance
(212) 909-2818

Company Description

Describe your firm's business and the types of clients served by your finance group(s).

CS First Boston Group, Inc. is a full-service global investment bank and securities firm working in close cooperation with Crédit Suisse. The company serves both suppliers and users of capital around the world and operates primarily through three wholly owned operating units: The First Boston Corporation in the Americas; CS First Boston Pacific, Inc. in the Asia/Pacific region; and Financière Crédit Suisse–First Boston in Europe, the Middle East, and Africa. Through these companies, CS First Boston Group, Inc. provides comprehensive financial advisory and capital-raising services and develops innovative financing for a broad range of clients. The firm employs its own capital resources to trade and underwrite securities. In addition, CS First Boston Group, Inc. has a 50% nonvoting common stock interest in Crédit Suisse Financial Products, a London-headquartered joint venture with Crédit Suisse, providing derivative product services worldwide.

In 1992 alone, we lead managed $98.7 billion in debt and equity issues and helped 134 merger and acquisition clients to complete transactions in 24 countries totaling $61 billion. In both worldwide privatization and merger and acquisition advisory areas, as well as in the underwriting of asset-backed securities, the CS First Boston Group ranked first in the annual standings.

Describe your ownership structure.

CS First Boston Group, Inc. is a privately owned company headquartered in New York. At year end, CS Holding, which owns the leading Swiss bank, Crédit Suisse, held a 66.13% economic interest in the common stock of CS First Boston Group, Inc. CS First Boston Group, Inc. employees held an 18.23% investment interest in the company, and a group of financial institutions from Japan, Europe, the Middle East, and America held the remaining 15.64%.

CS First Boston is a network of decentralized operating companies. Each company has a strong local market presence and market knowledge and is largely staffed by professionals indigenous to its area. Under the CS First Boston umbrella, these individual area strengths are combined to offer meaningful benefits—global reach and local expertise. More and more clients tell us that this structure enables CS First Boston to be more responsive to specific markets, products, and services.

The Finance MBA's Job Description

Describe the career path and corresponding responsibilities for an MBA at your firm.

Investment Banking
Upon joining First Boston, a new associate has the opportunity to learn about every department in the firm through a brief orientation program. Typically, investment banking associates spend their early years working in a given group or groups on a broad range of assignments that further their career development and reflect the demands of the marketplace. The goal is to expose our professionals to a rich variety of assignments and clients so that they will be well equipped to assume a higher level of client responsibility. We offer additional training through a series of ongoing work seminars conducted by professionals from inside and outside the firm.

Sales and Trading
The formal sales and trading program lasts approximately five months. It consists of intensive classroom instruction, reading assignments, and special projects. Each associate also engages in rotational assignments that expose the associate to the professionals in sales and trading and to their day-to-day activities. Upon successful completion of the training program, each associate is selected for a sales or trading position.

Public Finance
A new associate in First Boston's Public Finance Department is assigned to one of five industry groups based on the associate's interest and expertise and the needs of the department. New associates have the opportunity to be assigned to more than one industry group but generally specialize after two years. Exposure is gained through

work on financing teams, which typically consist of one vice president, the associate, and an analyst. An associate is responsible for all aspects of executing a given transaction under the supervision of a senior member of the financing team. Such training, supplemented by ongoing seminars, is critical in assuming greater client responsibility.

The Recruiting Process

Describe your recruiting process and the criteria by which you select candidates. Are grades a criterion? Is prior experience necessary?

First Boston seeks highly motivated individuals with demonstrated records of achievement who have the ability to work effectively with others, both clients and fellow professionals. First Boston investment bankers come from diverse backgrounds. They demonstrate initiative and relate well to both colleagues and clients. In addition, they enjoy working in an atmosphere that may be best described as collegial and constructive. Considerable resources are invested by the firm in developing the talents of these individuals in an effort to produce broadly skilled investment bankers.

Do you have a summer program for associates or analysts? If so, please describe.

First Boston's Summer Associate Program gives students finishing their first year of business school an opportunity to learn about investment banking, real estate, sales and trading, and public finance by participating in transactions, new business presentations, and rotational and analytical assignments. More than 50% of new permanent associates hired this year have had experience as Summer Associates or as postcollege Financial Analysts at First Boston.

Ford Motor Company

20000 Rotunda Drive
P.O. Box 2053
Scientific Research Lab
Dearborn, MI 48121
(313) 845-5366

MBA Recruiting Contact(s):
Jeff Hitchcock

Company Description

Describe your firm's business and the types of clients served by your finance group(s).

Ford is the world's fourth-largest industrial corporation and the second-largest producer of cars and trucks. It also ranks among the largest providers of financial services in the United States. Approximately 325,000 employees in our plants, offices, and laboratories serve the automotive and financial services needs of customers in more than 200 countries and territories.

Our two core businesses are the Automotive Group and the Financial Services Group, which consists of Ford Credit, The Associates, First Nationwide, and U.S. Leasing. We also are engaged in a number of other businesses, including electronics, glass, electrical and fuel-handling products, plastics, climate control systems, service and replacement parts, vehicle leasing and rental, and land development.

Our Finance Organization serves a broad range of internal and external clients. The primary focus of Finance at Ford is on providing timely and accurate financial analysis to company management in order to support a wide range of business decisions.

Describe your ownership structure.

Ford Motor Company is a widely held, publicly traded corporation. Approximately 40% of the voting shares in the corporation are controlled by the Class B stock—controlled by the Ford family.

How does your approach to finance differ from that of other firms, and what do you consider to be your strengths and distinctive capabilities?

Historically, finance has played a very strong role in the automobile industry, particularly at Ford. In fact, in a recent survey conducted by *CFO* magazine, over 200 financial executives, executive recruiters, bankers, and consultants identified Ford Motor Company as one of the three companies that best prepares financial managers for the chief financial officer chair.

Finance professionals are involved in every aspect of the company's operations—product development, engineering, sales and marketing, customer service (sale of aftermarket parts), and financial services—as well as the traditional finance functions, such as treasury, financial planning, and operations analysis. Typically, finance professionals move frequently among the company's different components, developing into well-rounded managers who can fill top-level positions in the Finance Organization or in general management. The extensive roster of Finance alumni in senior management includes Harold Poling, Chairman and Chief Executive Officer; Allan Gilmour, Vice Chairman; and Wayne Booker, Executive Vice President of International Automotive.

Finance MBAs at Ford can expect a wide variety of challenging assignments that expose them to all the functional areas of the corporation. At Ford, finance is not about abstract theories; it is about real decisions that affect the viability of a multi-billion-dollar new car platform, the investment in hundreds of millions of dollars' worth of plant and equipment, or the pricing strategy of a major product line.

The Finance MBA's Job Description

Describe the career path and corresponding responsibilities for an MBA at your firm.

The Career Foundation Development Program ensures an early diversity of experiences, with the following job rotations (and job responsibilities):

- Year 1: At a vehicle assembly plant or a component manufacturing plant, typically located in the Midwest (manufacturing cost analysis, operations analysis, and special projects).

- Years 2 and 3: At one of the following groups, generally located in Dearborn, MI:
    Product Development (develop proposals for new product programs, analyze product line profitability).
    Sales (establish pricing strategies and incentive programs for new and existing products, competitive analysis).

Treasury/Capital Markets (capital structure decisions for acquisitions/joint ventures, dividend policy for parent/foreign affiliates, issuance of debt/equity, foreign exchange).

Manufacturing General Offices (capital project analysis, e.g., review of plant expansion proposals and quality improvement actions).

Parts and Service (financial analysis related to sales of after-market parts).

Ford Motor Credit Company/Financial Services (funding of automotive receivables via asset-backed securities, commercial paper, and/or swaps).

- Year 4: Rotate to a new organization (one of the groups listed above). Future rotations could be expected about every two years.

After the Foundation Development Program, an MBA could become a supervisor, and eventually a Finance Manager or Plant Controller. Longer term, a career path could lead an MBA to become Controller of a division, to become Treasurer of an affiliate, or to move into general management.

Discuss the lifestyle aspects of a career with your firm (i.e., average hours per week, amount of travel, flexibility to change offices, corporate culture, etc.).

The finance culture at Ford is reflective of the people we hire: highly analytical, aggressive, motivated, and career oriented—with a strong desire to win. Professional development is an integral part of our corporate culture. At Ford, we view our people as an investment, not an expense.

Ford world headquarters is in Dearborn, MI, located about 15 miles from downtown Detroit. Southeastern Michigan offers a wide variety of affordable housing and an easy commute to the office yet has access to all of the cultural amenities one would expect of the nation's sixth largest metropolitan area, including outstanding universities, world-class museums, and four professional sports teams.

The Recruiting Process

Describe your recruiting process and the criteria by which you select candidates. Are grades a criterion? Is prior experience necessary?

Ford is looking for aggressive, intelligent, highly motivated men and women who are looking for a challenge in an exciting, highly competitive industry. As Ford enters the twenty-first century, we face many challenges: globalization, trade barriers, increased regulation, excess capacity, and stiff competition, to name a few. We are looking for people to help us meet these challenges.

Prior technical experience or education is helpful but certainly not essential. A healthy interest in, and a willingness to get close to, our products is more essential to long-term success at Ford.

Our recruiting process includes a recruiting briefing in the fall followed by on-campus interviews in the winter. On-site visits follow a successful on-campus interview. In addition we will arrange a visit for candidates to take a "Ford Finance Test Drive"—an opportunity to spend a day with an MBA who has worked at Ford for two or three years. He or she will show what a typical day is like. The Ford Finance Test Drive provides an additional opportunity to decide if Ford is the right place to make your career.

Do you have a summer program for associates or analysts? If so, please describe.

Ford plans to continue to seek a limited number of talented individuals for a variety of summer positions. Summer positions are designed to provide a challenging short-term assignment that will give an accurate perspective on a full-time career at Ford. The process and qualifications for summer applicants are similar to those for full-time positions.

What international opportunities does your firm offer for U.S. citizens? For foreign nationals?

Ford derives about 40% of its revenues from international operations, offering abundant opportunities for international experience. Overseas assignments, if desired, are possible after completion of the Foundation Development Program. Many Ford executives have had international experience at some point in their careers.

Ford recruits MBAs who are U.S. citizens or are authorized to work full time in the United States.

General Motors Corporation
New York Treasurer's Office

GM Building
767 Fifth Avenue
New York, NY 10153
(212) 418-6193

MBA Recruiting Contact(s):
Nick Hotchkin, HBS '93
Jeff Henderson, HBS '91
Richard Selvala, HBS '90

Company Description

Describe your firm's business and the types of clients served by your finance group(s).

General Motors designs, manufactures, and sells automobiles, trucks, vans, locomotives, and other equipment and components related to the worldwide transportation industry. In addition, the corporation is involved in the design and manufacture of satellites, integrated circuits, electronic-optical sensors, guidance systems, and other defense electronics systems, as well as financial services and the application of a wide range of computer systems and software.

The global automobile industry is progressing into an era of unprecedented competition. At General Motors, we are approaching this challenge with a commitment to remaining the premier manufacturer of cars and trucks in North America and the rest of the world. As has been well documented in the press, this commitment has resulted in a period of incredible change, with the entire GM organization being scrutinized and restructured. This process is placing emphasis on the ability of GM's employees to manage its operations and finance effectively.

GM's New York Treasurer's Office plays a vital role in the decisions that affect both the current operations of the corporation and its future direction. The office is extensively responsible for a broad range of financial, strategic planning, and other business matters leading to the execution of transactions, including new business ventures, domestic and international subsidiary financings, investments, divestitures, capital planning, and foreign exchange trading. In addition to developing and executing action plans for top management, the Treasurer's Office is also responsible for presenting such action plans and other information to the Board of Directors and its Finance, Audit, Incentive and Compensation, and Nominating Committees. As such, GM's New York Treasurer's Office distinguishes itself from other corporate treasury staffs by providing individuals with the opportunity to develop and practice corporate finance, consulting, and general management skills.

Furthermore, the appeal of the Treasurer's Office extends beyond that provided by traditional treasury functions. Specifically, GM's Treasurer's Office also functions as GM's in-house consulting firm. As such, the office's responsibilities include developing, assessing, negotiating, and implementing strategic business initiatives of the corporation. Reflecting the Treasurer's Office objectives of developing both the financial and general business acumen of its employees, many alumni have progressed to top financial and general management positions throughout the United States and virtually all of our international locations, including Europe, Asia, and South America.

The Finance MBA's Job Description

Describe the career path and corresponding responsibilities for an MBA at your firm.

A Senior Financial Analyst in the office is exposed to a wide range of strategic and financial assignments that can be matched by very few other companies. For example, a typical business school graduate could immediately be engaged in any of several activities, including structuring an international subsidiary or joint venture, developing an entirely new form of equity or debt offering, managing GM's multi-billion-dollar cash portfolio, or trading foreign currency on a global basis. Newly hired MBAs are provided with the opportunity to practice a wide range of corporate finance activities. In this regard, individuals in the Treasurer's Office are rotated from section to section in order to develop their breadth of expertise fully. Senior Analysts would typically follow a rotational assignment system through several of nine office sections, which places emphasis on developing general managers proficient in many areas of finance. While the responsibilities of each section and position vary, analysts are expected to develop a broad knowledge of GM's operations, its products, and its markets on a worldwide basis. Key responsibilities within the sections include:

- Business Development and Analysis
  —Business associations and partnerships
  —Acquisition and divestiture analysis and execution

- Corporate Financing and Investment
  —Capital structure and analysis
  —Capital planning
  —Cash portfolio management
  —Capital markets

- Investor Relations and Competitive Analysis
  —Communication with Wall Street analysts
  —Competitive analysis and intelligence

- Overseas Borrowings
  —Overseas capital planning and control
  —All non-U.S. financings

- Overseas Financial Analysis and Special Projects
  —Analysis and structuring of overseas joint ventures, acquisitions, and divestitures
  —Analysis of overseas subsidiary printability and investment proposals

- Worldwide Banking and U.S. Cash Management
  —Banking and domestic cash resources management

- Foreign Exchange, Commodities Futures, and International Cash Management
  —Foreign exchange analysis and hedging
  —Metals futures trading
  —Export financing
  —Overseas subsidiaries cash management

- Executive Compensation
  —Parent company and subsidiary incentive compensation design and analysis

- Employee Benefit Plans Analysis
  —National negotiations with the United Auto Workers Union
  —Domestic and international benefit plan design and analysis
  —Salaried and hourly labor cost analysis

- Regional Treasury Center (satellite office in Brussels, Belgium)
  —Foreign exchange and interest rate exposure
  —Management of GM's European Subsidiaries
  —Short-term funding requirements in Europe
  —Special project finance transactions

Outlined below are the job classifications within the New York Treasurer's Office and the average time it has historically taken qualified MBAs to attain these levels:

Job Classification	Average Time to Promotion
Senior Financial Analyst (entry-level position for MBA)	—
Manager (typically supervises 4 or 5 analysts)	2–3 years
Section Director (responsible for 1 or 2 managers and 7–9 analysts)	2 years
Assistant Treasurer	5 years

Describe the opportunities for professional mobility between the various departments in your firm.

In addition to promotions leading to a successful and rewarding experience at the Treasurer's Office in New York, numerous financial openings occur for Treasurer's Office employees at overseas and domestic subsidiaries and divisions (e.g., GM Hughes Electronics, NUMMI [GM's joint venture with Toyota in Fremont, CA], GMAC, Saturn, GM-Europe, EDS, and GM's North American Operations). Furthermore, many opportunities are available outside the financial side of the business, including general management, personnel, industrial relations, manufacturing, industry-government relations, and our worldwide trading corporation.

The Recruiting Process

Describe your recruiting process and the criteria by which you select candidates. Are grades a criterion? Is prior experience necessary?

GM's Treasurer's Office is staffed with approximately 60 MBAs from the nation's top schools and from around the globe. We seek individuals with initiative and a willingness to assume a demanding work load in a challenging environment, as new Analysts are expected to assume a significant amount of responsibility within a very short period of time. A typical Senior Financial Analyst has a strong academic background, with particular emphasis on finance; a background in economics, accounting, engineering, or operations is also valuable. Attractive candidates demonstrate strong analytical and organizational abilities, as well as effective oral and written communication skills. Importantly, they also have a high level of interpersonal skills and an ability to function effectively as part of a team.

Do you have a summer program for associates or analysts? If so, please describe.

GM's Treasurer's Office has an excellent summer program that allows students between years of business school to learn about the New York office and gain valuable knowledge and skills in a particular section. Many of our recent summer Analysts have elected to return to the Treasurer's Office upon graduating.

Goldman, Sachs & Co.

85 Broad Street
New York, NY 10004
(212) 902-1000

MBA Recruiting Contact(s):
David M. Darst, Vice President—Equities Division; for Equities Division and for Global Operations and Technology Division

Chris C. Casciato, Vice President—Investment Banking Division, and Jide J. Zeitlin, Vice President—Investment Banking Division; for Investment Banking Division and Principal Investment Area

Frank J. Gaul, Vice President—Fixed Income Division; for Fixed Income Division

Brian J. Duffy, Vice President—J. Aron Currency and Commodities Division; for J. Aron Currency and Commodities Division

Company Description

Describe your firm's business and the types of clients served by your finance group(s).

Goldman, Sachs & Co. is a full-service international investment banking and securities firm headquartered in New York City. Major offices in London and Tokyo serve as European and Asia/Pacific Basin headquarters, respectively. Other offices are located throughout the United States and in Frankfurt, Hong Kong, Montreal, Paris, Singapore, Sydney, Toronto, and Zurich.

The firm is a leader in virtually every aspect of financing and investing, serving corporations, institutions, governments, and individual clients. A recent survey of U.S. corporate financial officers named Goldman, Sachs the leading investment banking firm for overall service to large public companies. Another survey of U.S. chief financial officers and top institutional money managers names the firm "best broker" for the second consecutive year.

Our leadership derives principally from the dedication, talent, and professionalism of our people. We recruit and train the very best graduates from leading colleges and universities. These individuals become part of our noted team effort, which provides the closely integrated financial skills and services necessary to help our clients meet diverse goals and new challenges in global markets.

The following is a brief overview of the firm's organization and activities.

Investment Banking Division

The Investment Banking Division assists corporations, financial institutions, and governments in planning and executing financial strategies in the global capital markets.

Corporate Finance. Our Corporate Finance Department professionals concentrate the firm's resources on identifying alternative sources of capital and on developing innovative techniques to match the interests of users and providers of capital. Transactions, structured and executed worldwide, include public debt and equity offerings and private placements of debt and equity. The firm is a leading manager of public offerings in the United States and abroad and a major factor in arranging private financings. The firm is also active in corporate workouts and restructurings.

Energy and Telecommunications Group. The Energy and Telecommunications Group provides investment banking services to Goldman, Sachs's clients in four principal industries: Oil and Gas, Pipelines, Utilities, and Telecommunications.

Financial Institutions Group. Professionals in the Financial Institutions Group provide full-service investment banking services to many of the largest banks, insurance companies, money managers, finance companies, and thrift institutions worldwide.

Structured Finance Group. The Structured Finance Group is responsible for the conception, development, promotion, and execution of a variety of types of financing transactions characterized by nonconventional features. These features include noncorporate legal structures, advantageous tax or accounting treatment, nonconventional sources of capital, and contractual mechanics governing business input and output.

Mergers and Acquisitions. The Mergers and Acquisitions Department, consistently a leading advisor in major merger transactions, assists corporations in achieving financial and strategic objectives through sales, acquisition, divestitures, leveraged buyouts, and recapitalizations, and defending against hostile takeovers.

Capital Markets. Professionals in our Capital Markets Groups advise issuing clients on capital-raising strategies and opportunities by communicating current fixed income market and product information generated by our trading, sales, and foreign exchange professionals worldwide.

Real Estate. The Real Estate Department serves the world's leading corporations, real estate developers, and institutions. The firm is dominant in arranging sales and financings of investment-grade office, retail, hotel, industrial, and multifamily properties. These transactions frequently involve foreign investors and lenders and include capital markets instruments such as securitized offerings, interest rate swaps, and credit enhancements.

Investment Banking Services. The Investment Banking Services Department is the marketing arm of the Investment Banking Division. Professionals are responsible for maintaining and strengthening client relationships and developing new relationships and business. In cooperation with each execution department, professionals create and implement marketing plans for specific products as well as strategies to enhance the firm's overall presence and reputation worldwide.

Principal Investment Area

Principal Investment professionals are responsible for the principal investing activities of the firm, including the firm-sponsored investment funds. All principal investments are made so as not to conflict with client objectives.

Fixed-Income Division

The Fixed-Income Division serves investing and issuing clients as a leader in marketing and trading fixed income securities and derivative products in all major financial markets. A majority of the division's professionals are involved in sales, trading, and research. The division also includes Municipal Finance and Asset-Backed Finance professionals.

Sales and Trading. Sales and Trading professionals work within groups that concentrate on such specific fixed income products as government and agency securities, corporate securities, mortgage-backed securities, high-yield securities, municipal securities, futures and options, and preferred stock.

Sales professionals play a key role in the firm's capital markets transactions. They assist institutional investors in planning and implementing portfolio strategies. As a critical link between the firm's issuing and investing clients, they ensure the successful distribution of new issues and the firm's ability to underwrite the debt of corporations, governments, and other major borrowers.

Trading professionals make markets in major debt securities as well as in derivatives of those securities. They commit the firm's capital to ensure liquidity for investing clients. Traders are continually in touch with sales professionals, soliciting investor opinions and suggesting investment strategies. Traders also advise capital markets, investment banking, and syndicate professionals on the pricing, structuring, and timing of new issues, as well as on debt repurchase, synthetic securities, and asset swaps.

Fixed Income Research. The Fixed Income Research Department uses sophisticated analytical, mathematical, and computer capabilities to develop new ideas, products, and approaches for trading, hedging, and investment strategies as well as for asset-liability management. Professionals work in specialized sections covering debt options, trading systems, asset-liability management, risk management, sales support, financial modeling, hedging, portfolio optimization, new product development, and research.

Municipal Finance. Professionals in our Municipal Finance Department are responsible for developing new business opportunities, structuring and executing transactions, and providing ongoing financial advisory services for issuers of municipal bonds. Clients include states, state agencies, local governments, hospitals, health care systems, airports, public power authorities, colleges and universities, housing finance agencies, mass transit systems, and cultural institutions. The department originates and underwrites the full spectrum of tax-exempt and taxable municipal debt, ranging from tax-exempt commercial paper, variable-rate demand notes, and put bonds, to long-term, fixed-rate bonds.

Asset-Backed Finance. Our Asset-Backed Finance professionals—who are part of the Mortgage Securities Department—provide a full range of investment banking services to clients, including thrift institutions, mortgage bankers, federal agencies, home builders, commercial banks, and insurance, finance, and industrial companies.

Equities Division

Through its Equities Division, Goldman, Sachs underwrites, distributes, and trades equity securities and derivative products on a worldwide basis. Goldman, Sachs' position in the global equities marketplace results from its product innovation, distribution capability, and willingness to commit capital in response to clients' needs. The division has long-standing relationships with a wide range of institutional investors and wealthy family groups.

As a member of the New York, London, Frankfurt, and Tokyo stock exchanges, Goldman, Sachs is a trader and market maker in U.S., European, U.K., Japanese, and other global equities. Trading and execution activities are conducted as both agent and principal.

Institutional Investor Services. The Institutional Investor Services Department provides trading and research coverage, through product-focused specialists, to institutional clients, including public and private pension funds, insurance companies, mutual funds, hedge funds, banks, investment advisors, endowments, and foundations in the United States, Europe, and Asia.

Global Convertible Securities. The Global Convertible Securities Department distributes, makes markets, and conducts arbitrage in U.S., yen-denominated, and Euroconvertible bonds and in a substantial portion of U.S.-convertible preferred stocks. Equity warrants specialists in New York, London, and Tokyo make markets and conduct arbitrage in U.S., Japanese, and European warrant issues.

Equity Derivatives. The Equity Derivatives Department distributes and trades listed and unlisted options and futures on market indexes, industry groups, and individual companies. The department develops quantitative strategies to effect portfolio hedging and restructuring, asset allocation, equity index swaps, and the construction of synthetic instruments. These instruments enable sophisticated investors to undertake desired hedging strategies and establish or liquidate investment positions not otherwise available in the financial markets.

Equity Capital Markets. The Equity Capital Markets Department advises corporate and governmental clients worldwide with regard to equity financing opportunities, privatization strategies, capital structure, and equity product design. Through the Equity Capital Markets Department, Goldman, Sachs manages international equity offerings, U.S. common stock offerings, and issues of ADRs by international companies.

Private Client Services. The Private Client Services Department provides comprehensive equity, fixed income, and cash management services, as well as securities safekeeping, margin lending, portfolio reporting, and principal investment opportunities to wealthy family groups, medium-size institutions, corporations, and professional investors worldwide.

Investment Research. The Investment Research Department consists of more than 80 analysts, located in New York, London, Frankfurt, and Tokyo, who provide quantitative and qualitative analyses of global economic, currency, and financial market trends; portfolio strategy;

asset allocation recommendations; industry weighting; and investment options on 1300 companies in over 80 different industries in the United States, Japan, Europe, and elsewhere.

J. Aron Currency and Commodity Division
The J. Aron Currency and Commodity Division, with offices in New York, London, Tokyo, and Singapore, is a leading market maker in foreign exchange and commodities worldwide, providing complete trading, hedging, and advisory services to corporations, institutions, and governments. The division's activities include:

> Foreign Exchange Trading Department
> Foreign Exchange Sales Department
> Oil and Natural Gas Trading Department
> Coffee Trading Department
> Grain Trading Department
> Metals Trading Department
> Currency and Commodity Investment Products
>   Department

Global Operations and Technology Division
Integral roles in firmwide activities are played by our information technologies, securities operations, controllers, credit, treasury, and personnel professionals.

Information Technologies. Information Technologies serves the business, operations, and administrative areas of the firm by managing the delivery of high-quality computer systems.

Controllers. The Controllers Department designs and monitors all internal financial functions. The department is responsible for internal financial analysis and consulting, external financial reporting, monitoring internal trading positions and regulatory compliance, and general accounting for the firm.

Credit. The Credit Department approves and monitors the credit/exposure limits of many companies with which Goldman, Sachs does business. The department participates in the solicitation, structuring, and selling of commercial paper and conducts due diligence investigations.

Treasury. Worldwide funding of the firm's operations is the responsibility of the Treasury Department. The firm is rated A1 + , the highest ranking for commercial paper issuers assigned by Standard & Poor's.

Personnel. Our Personnel professionals ensure that Goldman, Sachs maintains the highest standards in all human resources activities. Functional areas include benefits and compensation, employment and employee relations, training and professional development, personnel systems and administration, and international personnel operations.

Describe your ownership structure.

Founded in 1869, Goldman, Sachs is the only remaining private partnership among the major Wall Street organizations. Our partnership structure fosters a culture that is characterized by teamwork, aggressive pursuit of business opportunities, compensation that is commensurate with responsibility and performance, and sound financial management. We have historically been among the most profitable investment banking firms.

How does your approach to finance differ from that of other firms, and what do you consider to be your strengths and distinctive capabilities?

Commitment to client interests and teamwork are the most distinctive characteristics of our approach to investment banking. We emphasize relationships rather than the completion of individual transactions. Our success is directly related to our ability to provide our clients with exceptional service. Among our key strengths are the following:

The skill, experience, and dedication of our people.
Leadership in financial markets worldwide.
Strong capital position.
Technological resources.
Reputation for excellence.

Most important, we believe our ability to integrate all facets of the firm's areas of excellence through teamwork is unique in the industry.

The Finance MBA's Job Description

Describe the career path and corresponding responsibilities for an MBA at your firm.

The firm recruits MBAs for career positions in all divisions and operating entities. Initial training will depend on the new Associate's background and functional area. Training emphasizes on-the-job learning, which is complemented by formal instruction. Professionals throughout the firm serve as instructors and mentors. During training, Associates prepare for any registration exams that may be required for their specialization. They begin training in their functional areas after they complete those exams. Associates are encouraged to assume as much responsibility in their assignments as they can handle.

Associates play an integral role in planning, structuring, and executing transactions that range from a single private placement of equity or debt to a major portfolio restructuring or corporate reorganization. They work with Partners, Vice Presidents, other Associates, and Analysts in an open atmosphere in which ideas are shared and creative thinking is encouraged. Because the firm has only three levels of professionals, new Associates have significant contact with its senior members.

Describe the opportunities for professional mobility between the various departments in your firm.

As part of career development, we foster a working environment in which professionals are encouraged to explore their interests and develop their skills continuously. Believing that diversity of experience is beneficial not only to our professionals but also to the firm and its clients, we provide opportunities to work in other areas of the firm and to transfer to other departments, divisions, or offices.

We are diligent in evaluating professionals for career advancement and financial reward. Yearly reviews are made by teams of superiors and peers to ensure thoroughness and objectivity.

Discuss the lifestyle aspects of a career with your firm (i.e., average hours per week, amount of travel, flexibility to change offices, corporate culture, etc.).

A career at Goldman, Sachs is a challenging one that places significant demands on time and energy. Professionals are encouraged to make their lifestyle decisions within the context of doing the best job possible. The amount of travel varies greatly. In areas requiring the most travel, our professionals can average two or three days on the road each week.

As a result of our care in hiring, developing, challenging, and rewarding our people, the turnover rate for our professionals has consistently been one of the lowest in the industry.

The Recruiting Process

Describe your recruiting process and the criteria by which you select candidates. Are grades a criterion? Is prior experience necessary?

In recruiting, we look for professionals who will flourish in a team-oriented environment. There is no single type of individual who fits in at Goldman, Sachs. We are an amalgam of people from around the world with different cultural and educational backgrounds and professional orientations. What we have in common are creativity, the confidence and willingness to take initiative and responsibility, an interest in being a part of a highly motivated group, and a desire to achieve beyond the norm.

Although each area of specialization requires certain qualities, most of our professionals demonstrate a keen interest in the financial markets; strong interpersonal, analytic, and communication skills; and an ability to respond creatively and quickly in a fast-paced, changing environment.

We believe that academic achievement is a good indication of potential, but it is not the most important criterion. Prior experience is usually not a major consideration for MBAs.

In a typical year, how many permanent associates and analysts do you hire? Do you have a summer program for associates or analysts? If so, please describe.

We offer a two-year financial analyst program for college graduates. Each year, we hire a significant number of college graduates in the Investment Banking Division worldwide. In addition, there are select analyst positions elsewhere in the firm. As with MBAs, most of the training of college graduates is on the job. Many of our analysts earn an MBA and return to the firm as Associates. The contact for the program is Andrea Baum, Investment Banking Division (212) 902-0003.

The firm actively recruits for its Summer Associate program. Our Summer Associates gain broad exposure to many areas of our business, and many return as full-time employees.

What international opportunities does your firm offer for U.S. citizens? For foreign nationals?

Investment banking has become an international business, and Goldman, Sachs is fully committed to the business on a worldwide basis. In addition to our headquarters in New York City, we have major offices in London and Tokyo, which serve as our European and Asian/Pacific Basin headquarters, respectively. We have other offices located throughout the United States, as well as Frankfurt, Hong Kong, Montreal, Paris, Singapore, Sydney, Toronto, and Zurich. Consequently, we offer many international opportunities for both U.S. citizens and foreign nationals.

Hewlett-Packard Company

3000 Hanover Street
Palo Alto, CA 94304

MBA Recruiting Contact(s):
George Chung
175 Wyman Street
Waltham, MA 02254
(617) 290-3025

Company Description

Describe your firm's business and the types of clients served by your finance group(s).

Hewlett-Packard (HP) is a leading international manufacturer of computing and electronic measuring equipment for people in business, industry, science, engineering, health care, and education. The company's more than 12,000 products include computers and peripheral products, test and measuring instruments and computerized test systems, networking products, electronic components, hand-held calculators, medical electronic equipment, and instruments and systems for chemical analysis.

HP's basic business purpose is to help accelerate the advancement of knowledge and fundamentally improve the effectiveness of people and organizations worldwide.

Describe your ownership structure.

HP is a publicly owned company and is one of the 40 largest industrial corporations in America. HP stock is traded on the New York Stock Exchange.

How does your approach to finance differ from that of other firms, and what do you consider to be your strengths and distinctive capabilities?

HP's combination of strength and structure enables us to offer a broad spectrum of financial career opportunities and early responsibility.

HP's unique corporate culture, often referred to as the "HP Way," is a combination of organizational values, corporate objectives, and company practices. The company is built upon values such as honesty, teamwork, and respect that are reflected in everything we do.

One of our guiding objectives as a company is profit. The profit we generate from our operations is the ultimate source of the funds we need to prosper and grow. It is the one absolutely essential measure of our corporate performance over the long term. Without profit, the company is unable to grow or fulfill the rest of its objectives.

Our long-standing policy has been to reinvest most of our profits and to depend on this reinvestment, plus funds from employee stock purchases and other cash flow items, to finance our growth.

The day-to-day performance of each individual adds to—or subtracts from—our profit. Profit is seen as the responsibility of all HP employees.

Discuss changes in your firm's revenues (both domestic and international) and professional staff over the past year; over the past five years.

In fiscal year 1992, ending October 31, 1992, net revenues rose 13% to $16.4 billion, following a 10% increase in fiscal year 1991.

HP employs approximately 92,600 people.

The Finance MBA's Job Description

Describe the career path and corresponding responsibilities for an MBA at your firm.

Financial Analyst positions are typically in HP product divisions, field sales organizations, or corporate functions. These initial experiences lead to careers in financial management or in other functional areas such as marketing and manufacturing.

In the divisions, Financial Analysts work closely with other functional areas. Tasks may include product/process cost analysis, financial planning and reporting, product pricing and profitability analysis, asset evaluation, and the design and implementation of financial models that will simulate division operations.

Financial Analysts in the sales regions are responsible for financial planning and reporting, customer leasing arrangements, credit analysis and accounts receivable management, inventory analysis and control, and contracts and order administration.

In our corporate headquarters, responsibilities may include many of the activities described above plus cash, debt, and foreign exchange management; pensions and investment analysis; coordination of long-range plans; the development of corporate financial policy; external shareholder and Securities and Exchange Commission reporting; and internal audit tasks.

Describe the opportunities for professional mobility between the various departments in your firm.

The company is committed to giving people the flexibility to reach well-defined goals. HP believes that freedom encourages the creativity and initiative of every employee. Career paths are not defined formally at HP; rather, they are flexible by design. We strive to help our people succeed and move on to greater challenges and responsibilities. An extensive internal job posting system allows employees to change jobs within their site (both within their function and across functions) and to move to other sites.

Discuss the lifestyle aspects of a career with your firm (i.e., average hours per week, amount of travel, flexibility to change offices, corporate culture, etc.).

HP trusts individuals and believes that people are committed to doing a good job given the right environment. To create this environment, HP offers pay based on performance, pleasant and open work environments, flexible work hours, cash profit sharing, and recognition for achievement.

The Recruiting Process

Describe your recruiting process and the criteria by which you select candidates. Are grades a criterion? Is prior experience necessary?

HP recruits highly motivated, successful MBAs with initiative and a strong desire to make a significant impact on our business. Prior experience is preferred although not mandatory. Candidates must have a thorough knowledge of financial and accounting principles and proficiency in PC-based analytical tools. We look for outstanding analytical and problem-solving ability, as well as flexibility and excellent communication skills.

In a typical year, how many permanent associates and analysts do you hire? Do you have a summer program for associates or analysts? If so, please describe.

The number of openings varies from year to year, but we typically have several Finance openings distributed among many of our operations.

HP's Student Employment and Educational Development (SEED) Program enables students who have completed their first year in business school to gain hands-on experience as contributing members of our Finance team.

What international opportunities does your firm offer for U.S. citizens? For foreign nationals?

Overseas employment opportunities are limited to foreign nationals.

50

IBM Corporation

One Copley Place
Boston, MA 02116
(617) 638-1907

MBA Recruiting Contact(s):
Ralph E. Barisano

Company Description

Describe your firm's business and the types of clients served by your finance group(s).

IBM is a unique organization—a major multinational corporation that takes pride in its small-team atmosphere.

Consider that the company stands at the leading edge of one of the world's most dynamic industries: information processing. Consider that it does business in over 130 countries.

Consider, also, that IBM is an organization known worldwide for its respect for the individual and its environment for personal and professional growth. Consider that it is a market-driven company dedicated to providing the best possible customer service and that it is committed to excellence in all activities. Consider that it is a dynamic organization constantly striving to be competitive, to be responsive, to push decision making down to manageable levels.

In fact, IBM is a number of things. It is products and services designed to help customers solve problems through the application of information solutions. It is mainframe, mid-range, and personal computer systems; software for systems, applications, communications, and application development; telecommunications products; office systems; and related supplies and services. All are products and services designed to help record, process, store, retrieve, and communicate information.

In addition, IBM is a technological leader—an innovator with over 32,000 patents worldwide and major contributions at all levels of information processing. The company invented FORTRAN, RAMAC, the floppy disk, the relational database concept, systems network architecture, RISC technology, and much more. It has continually increased the density of circuit packaging, recently producing the first 4-million-bit chip. IBM scientists have earned Nobel Prizes for advances in superconductivity and scan-ning tunneling microscopy. The company is exploring sub-half-micron lithography, optical storage, speech recognition, artificial intelligence—and a host of other technologies.

But IBM is also open communications channels and respect for privacy, career flexibility and promotion on merit, personal growth and recognition, shared employee/company responsibility, a balance of work and personal life, corporate citizenship, and a benefits program considered one of the finest in industry. In other words, IBM is a special place to work.

Within IBM, Finance is its own team, a function that cuts across organizational lines. A cadre of over 5,000 professionals in the United States, IBM Finance offers opportunities at U.S. plant, laboratory, marketing, and subsidiary locations, as well as at headquarters facilities. Joint ventures and business alliances are also mutually staffed with an IBM and partner financial team.

Working in IBM Finance, you will gain exposure to all aspects of the business. Financial decisions affect research, engineering, manufacturing, programming, marketing, administration, personnel, communications—all the basic functions of the company. As a member of an IBM financial team, you will be in frequent contact with senior management early in your career. From the start, you will also interact with your counterparts at other locations.

In the process, you will gain an understanding of the business and what makes it work. To build a career in IBM Finance, you need a perspective that cuts across functional lines. A pricing decision in Raleigh, NC, can affect accounting controls in Boca Raton, FL. Financial planning for the IBM Credit Corporation can affect the treasury function at corporate headquarters in Armonk, NY. Equity investments can have worldwide implications.

The Finance MBA's Job Description

Describe the career path and corresponding responsibilities for an MBA at your firm.

Career paths in IBM Finance are characterized by a variety of experience and responsibilities, with advancement on merit. The path you follow depends on your objectives and how well you do in the variety of job responsibilities you will be given. You can move ahead as fast as your capabilities permit.

You will most likely start in financial planning or accounting—with later assignments in these areas plus pricing, treasury, and controllership—and rotate assignments for balanced experience. You could start as a Cost Accounting Analyst, become a Planning Manager, move on to be a Product Pricer in an international headquarters in Paris—all while moving up in your career. An assignment in the IBM Credit Corporation might be in the picture. Ideally, your performance will lead you to first-line management in an operation unit, then on toward executive positions in financial or general management or increased professional staff responsibility.

Throughout your career, training will be largely on the job, enriched by formal classroom work within and outside the company. In fact, your training and education will never stop.

Looking Ahead with Financial Planning

A major entry-level area is financial planning—the development of basic financial strategies by which IBM runs its business. Financial planning is to IBM management what flowcharting is to the programmer. It establishes short-range projections of income and expense—the operating plan—and long-range strategic planning for the business environment.

IBM financial planning starts with determination of the goals and objectives of the business deliberately set at challenging but realistically attainable levels. Basic inputs are the following: customer requirements, competitive analysis, industry opportunity, technology trends, and available resources (both dollars and people). From goals and objectives, financial planners develop strategies for the business. This demands analysis of the company's current position and the availability of alternate strategies for the future.

In this area, you will work hand-in-hand with the IBM engineering, manufacturing, marketing, and general management communities to understand requirements, analyze IBM's and competitors' strengths and weaknesses, and realistically assess opportunities. You will interact closely with product planners; forecasters; and development, marketing, and service organizations. You may develop business models with desired returns, do portfolio analysis, or make investment decisions.

Aside from overall short- and long-term evaluations, your work can extend to specific IBM lines of business. Here the focus is on discrete markets and products, including the impact of competition. Developing, implementing, and controlling IBM financial plans calls for rigorous objectivity. Every recommendation must be judged by one basic criterion: Is this a sound business decision for IBM?

Financial planning at IBM helps convert goals to reality. Your experience in this area can make a real difference. You will develop creative ability, business judgment, and strong communications skills.

Accounting: The Language of the Business

A function of the office of the controller, accounting also offers a range of opportunities. State-of-the-art tools and technologies are used to collect, record, and report the company's economic transactions; the accountant's skills are used to interpret past business performance and to present recommendations for management decisions. The function is highly communications-oriented, with data consolidated from many sources for analysis and reporting in commonly understood terms.

Accounting fills many roles at IBM, from measurements and planning to government reporting and preparation of financial statements. Schedules are sensitive and demanding, logistics complex. The work demands teamwork and communication. You must accurately record financial results, comply with government regulations, and report earnings in a variety of ways. You must also ensure consistent presentation of accounting data and compliance with generally accepted accounting principles.

Accounting plays a vital, creative role in the management decision-making process at IBM. In an accounting position, you not only affect all basic operational areas—engineering, programming, marketing, administration—but also play a key role with IBM Treasury, international operations, and internal business partnership arrangements.

IBM also offers internal education to help you prepare for and take the Certified Management Accountant (CMA) exams. IBM is a corporate leader in the number of CMA certificates in its financial ranks.

IBM Pricing: Much More Than Finance

The pricing of IBM products and services is one of the most important responsibilities of the business. It is much more than finance—it is business itself. To ensure an adequate profit and return on investment, the pricing function must manage a product or service throughout its life, from conception to withdrawal from the market.

In simple terms, the role of pricing is to select IBM offerings and their prices to maximize the corporation's profitability. The major challenge is to ensure recovery of all costs and expenses, direct or indirect, associated with the development, manufacture, marketing, and maintenance of IBM products and services. In addition, IBM hardware, software, and service offerings must be understood within the context of a global marketplace where product strategies vary from country to country.

In fact, the pricing area is instrumental in initial selection of IBM products to be developed. Pricing Analysts work side by side with the product management and marketing teams to ensure that new product offerings will meet the needs of IBM customers. The pricing function takes a financial and general management role in the decision about a program's financial viability and match to IBM's strategic objectives.

Pricing has an impact on all stages of a product's life. In the introduction stage, price selection, and terms and conditions involve detailed analysis of several areas: business area opportunity, product function, strategy, positioning, price elasticity, supply constraints, cost trends in technologies, manufacturing process, research and development strengths, marketing support plans, and selection of cost-effective distribution channels. The product must be positioned with respect to competition, with respect to the needs of the customer, and within IBM's product line.

Once introduced, a product is open to competitive moves: new products, price cuts, discounting, creative marketing, and promotional tactics. Pricing's responsibility is to anticipate these actions and prepare appropriate responses. During the growth stage of the product life cycle, the generation of sales is paramount. This often means that competitive bid situations, existing prices, terms, conditions, and methodologies are constantly subject to review and fine tuning.

If you work in this area, you will draw on the full repertoire of financial skills acquired in business school. You will coordinate the efforts of many groups, including product managers, market requirements specialists, business planning managers, and product forecasters. It is a unique opportunity for cross-disciplinary exposure within IBM and excellent experience in the IBM Finance career.

Treasury: Providing Capital for the Business

The IBM Treasury function is responsible for managing the company's capital structure and securing funds needed to operate the business. This demands reliable forecasting of cash receipts and disbursements, up-to-the-minute knowledge of international money markets, selection of funding vehicles, and maintenance of relationships with investment banking and commercial banking institutions.

In effect, Treasury is a focal point for the evaluation of a broad range of complex financial alternatives. IBM is concerned with worldwide liquidity, asset safety, currency management, tax optimization and compliance, risk/insurance management, optimal capital structure, investor perceptions, portfolio returns, and cost of capital.

The worldwide nature of IBM's business also requires techniques to protect the company from fluctuation in the value of foreign currencies. The ultimate objective is to optimize the use of cash, to keep any excess funds appropriately invested until needed, and to ensure access to funds when needed at the most favorable terms possible.

Other activities within the Treasury organization include internal audit, retirement fund management, short-term investment supervision, intercompany relations, and IBM's corporate citizenship programs.

Opportunities in the IBM Credit Corporation

Opportunities are also available for recent graduates in the IBM Credit Corporation, a wholly owned corporate subsidiary. By helping customers acquire IBM products and services through competitive financing offerings, IBM Credit plays a pivotal role in providing complete customer solutions.

IBM Credit provides leases and other financing products, remarketing services, end-of-lease options, and—for IBM Business Partners—inventory financing programs. It also provides IBM employees with financial services such as a money market account and mutual funds.

IBM Credit contributes significantly to the corporation's competitiveness and to the growth and stability of IBM earnings.

Since IBM Credit's products are financing offerings, financial professionals are involved in every stage of product development and delivery. These stages include the following:

- Development of new financial offerings that respond to customer requirements and competitive opportunities.

- Assessments of credit risk and recovery of investment in high-risk situations.

- Pricing of specific customer proposals for financing, including unique terms and conditions and competitive tactics.

- Borrowing of debt funds via commercial paper, medium-term notes, and bond issues; relationships with investment-banking advisors.

- Managing capital structure, including asset and liability matching and relations with the principal rating agencies.

- Planning, accounting, and modeling financial performance, including publication of annual reports and supporting external financial communications.

The Recruiting Process

Describe your recruiting process and the criteria by which you select candidates. Are grades a criterion? Is prior experience necessary?

Within this environment, IBM Finance needs talented people with MBA degrees. The qualities sought are leadership, intelligence and awareness, interpersonal skills, creativity and ingenuity, energy, business maturity and judgment, integrity, personal enthusiasm, a goal-setting outlook, a desire to compete among the best—and the ability to be yourself.

The International Finance Corporation

1818 H Street, NW
Room I-2193
Washington, DC 20433
(202) 473-7972

MBA Recruiting Contact(s):
Cornelis de Kievit, Manager, Recruitment

Company Description

Describe your firm's business and the types of clients served by your finance group(s).

IFC seeks to carry out its mandate—helping developing nations achieve sustained economic growth—by supporting private sector development. It proves this support through three types of operations.

Project Financing
The most traditional of IFC's operations, project financing is also the largest. IFC commits over $1 billion in new project financing yearly. IFC finances the creation of new companies, as well as the expansion or modernization of established companies in virtually all sectors, from agribusiness to manufacturing to energy and mining. A significant number of projects backed by IFC, intended to help developing countries build up their financial sectors, involve the creation of institutions such as investment banks and venture capital, insurance, and leasing companies, as well as other specialized enterprises. IFC also provides lines of credit to financial intermediary institutions for onlending to enterprises too small to be the object of a direct investment by IFC. The Africa Enterprise Fund (AEF) directly finances small and midsize projects in sub-Saharan Africa.

The type of financial package provided by IFC is tailored to project requirements—IFC can provide loans, equity and quasi-equity, and guarantees, or a combination of these. Loans are offered at commercial rates with maturities and terms that vary with the needs of client companies. IFC finances only projects unable to obtain adequate funding from other sources and typically limits its loan or investment to 25% of total project costs, as it seeks not to replace private investment but to catalyze it. IFC does not accept government guarantees; it shares project risks with its investment partners. Before going

ahead with a project, IFC undertakes a thorough technical, financial, and economic appraisal to verify that the project is viable and likely to benefit the economy of the host country.

Mobilization of Finance
IFC mobilizes funds from other investors and lenders in a variety of ways. It actively seeks partners for joint ventures and raises additional finance for the projects in which it has invested, either by encouraging other institutions to make loans or equity investments in parallel to its own or by arranging syndicated loans for groups of commercial banks.

IFC also raises capital for companies in developing countries in the international financial markets by underwriting security offerings and by promoting vehicles for foreign portfolio investment such as country funds. IFC's in-house financial engineering expertise is applied to designing innovative financial products such as swaps, options, and convertible instruments to mobilize needed risk capital.

Advisory Services and Technical Assistance
Advisory services and technical assistance are frequently provided in the context of IFC's project-related activities. In the course of conducting project appraisals, for instance, IFC may provide technical assistance to project sponsors. IFC may also help in finding foreign partners, structuring transactions, and facilitating negotiations between foreign and domestic financiers and governments.

IFC provides advisory services to both government and corporate clients independently of project finance. IFC's Capital Markets Department advises member governments on the establishment of fiscal, legal, and regulatory frameworks that support the development of a market-oriented financial sector. IFC's Corporate Finance Services Department provides advice, often on a fee-earning basis, to private companies with heavy debt-servicing burdens on balance sheet restructuring, as well as to state-owned companies undergoing privatization. The Foreign Investment Advisory Service, operated jointly by IFC and the Multilateral Investment Guarantee Agency (MIGA), another member of the World Bank Group, advises member governments on policies, regulations, and institutions that can help them attract more foreign direct investment to priority sectors.

The Africa and Caribbean Project Development Facilities (APDF and CPDF), established in collaboration with the United Nations Development Programme

55

(UNDP) and other donor organizations, provide technical assistance to entrepreneurs in regions seeking to develop bankable projects and obtain financing. IFC recently established a similar facility for the South Pacific (SPPF).

The Finance MBA's Job Description

Describe the career path and corresponding responsibilities for an MBA at your firm.

As an IFC staff member, you will be part of a team of highly qualified and motivated professionals from around the world seeking creative—and profitable—solutions to complex business problems. You will face the challenges and earn the satisfactions of helping to further economic progress in the developing world through private sector development. And you will be working for a unique institution: IFC has a businesslike approach to development and believes that development and profitability go hand in hand.

Each staff member's performance is reviewed annually. Opportunities to maintain and expand individual skills are provided through an in-house training program particularly in technical subjects, finance, communications, and office technology.

IFC's more than 600 staff members come from about 70 different countries, including over 50 developing countries.

Discuss the lifestyle aspects of a career with your firm (i.e., average hours per week, amount of travel, flexibility to change offices, corporate culture, etc.).

Staff normally join IFC on regular appointments with no time limit, although appointments for a fixed term can also be arranged. The majority of staff are based in Washington, DC. Operational staff are likely to spend about one-fourth of their time on overseas travel.

The Recruiting Process

Describe your recruiting process and the criteria by which you select candidates. Are grades a criterion? Is prior experience necessary?

In addition to outstanding academic and professional qualifications, IFC's work requires creativity, flexibility, and imagination. Staff members are expected to take initiative and make sound independent judgments. Tact and sensitivity are critical, as staff will be working with private and public sector officials from many countries, often in very different cultural settings. Fluency and the ability to write cogently in English are required, and working knowledge of another language, particularly French, Spanish, Portuguese, Arabic, or Chinese, is an added advantage. Computer literacy is highly desirable.

IFC recruits professional staff on an international basis. The selection process is very competitive. Many of the professionals recruited by IFC are already in mid-career. However, IFC also recruits directly from leading business schools around the world to fill the growing number of openings for investment and financial officers. Recruitment teams visit a number of schools each year to conduct on-campus interviews. IFC is interested in interviewing MBA candidates in their last year of school who have at least a few years of experience relevant to IFC's needs and requirements.

J. & W. Seligman & Co. Incorporated

130 Liberty Street
New York, NY 10006
(212) 850-1864

MBA Recruiting Contact(s):
Jennifer Kovetz
(212) 488-0281

Company Description

Describe your firm's business and the types of clients served by your finance group(s).

J. & W. Seligman & Co. Incorporated was established in 1864 and since then has been providing financial services to individual and institutional investors. In its early years the firm was active in international finance, underwrote government and corporate securities, and handled investment and brokerage transactions of almost every type. In 1929 the firm established Tri-Continental, which today is one of the largest and oldest closed-end equity investment companies. The firm has been providing separate institutional, solely discretionary management since 1957. Today, our institutional clients include the New York City Police Pension Fund, the New York City Firefighters Pension Fund, the State of New York, State of Utah Retirement Systems, Louisiana State Employee Retirement System, California State Teachers Retirement System, and District of Columbia Retirement Board.

Describe your ownership structure.

The firm is owned by its active employees. Ownership in the firm is available to those who contribute to our clients and to the firm's long-term growth. In December 1988, the firm was recapitalized by a group of its present directors and William C. Morris. There are currently ten directors. We do not expect any changes in the near future, with the possible exception of adding new employee shareholders.

How does your approach to finance differ from that of other firms, and what do you consider to be your strengths and distinctive capabilities?

J. & W. Seligman & Co. Incorporated has a 128-year tradition of service to investors. Few other firms have remained independent for such a long period, and even fewer have had the kind of focus Seligman has had for the last 60 years. In a era of high-tech money management approaches, complex computer models, programmed trading, and extensive product proliferation, Seligman remains a company that has been consistent with an emphasis on personal service, thoroughness, professionalism, and superior long-term performance.

In addition to expanding our businesses, many of the companies in which we invest also help spur economic growth, enhance productivity, create new jobs, improve the environment, and provide more economical health care for more people. Our investment philosophy focuses on growth companies with an emphasis on value. We will invest only at a price that we believe does not reflect a company's long-term potential.

Our firm is owned by our active employees. In this regard, employees benefit directly when clients benefit from superior performance and asset growth. This has also resulted in a history of low turnover of personnel and in a consistent investment approach. Our professional staff is also motivated by a compensation structure that includes base salary, incentive compensation based on a percentage of the firm's profits, special compensation bonuses to reward individual achievement, a profit-sharing program, and a retirement income plan.

Discuss changes in your firm's revenues (both domestic and international) and professional staff over the past year; over the past five years.

In December 1988, we purchased the stock of a number of professionals who wished to retire or to leave the firm. These departures were planned, and staff was in place to succeed them. There have been five professional staff departures and seven additions over the last three years. However, the five departures were a result of our recapitalization. The firm had very few departures in the ten years prior to 1989.

Since 1980 we have grown from $2 billion in assets under management to approximately $10 billion today. During this period, our employees increased to approximately 270. Our plans are to continue to grow in both the separate account and mutual fund management areas.

The Finance MBA's Job Description

Describe the career path and corresponding responsibilities for an MBA at your firm. Describe the opportunities for professional mobility between the various departments of your firm.

Each newly hired Finance MBA (Investment Associate) will enter a flexible program designed to give the individual experience in the three key areas of the investment management business. Each Associate will be assigned to meaningful, hands-on projects in portfolio management and investment research, marketing, and general management and administration. The assignment in each of these functional areas will last 6 months. At the end of this 18-month program, each Associate will be assigned to a permanent position in one of these areas.

Discuss the lifestyle aspects of a career with your firm (i.e., average hours per week, amount of travel, flexibility to change offices, corporate culture, etc.).

A career with J. & W. Seligman & Co. Incorporated begins and continues with hard work and dedication to our unchanging philosophy. From Managing Directors on down, a commitment to service and product excellence exists. To achieve this goal but without sacrificing health and family, employees may work overtime and occasional weekends. Out-of-town travel is usually reserved for the senior managers although not uncommon for others.

The Recruiting Process

Describe your recruiting process and the criteria by which you select candidates. Are grades a criterion? Is prior experience necessary?

Prior applicable experience, especially entrepreneurial experience, is helpful. We look for the independent thinker and team player; superior oral communication skills including the ability to ask penetrating questions; solid accomplishments as a leader and managerial self-image; a high interest in the investment business as well as long-term goals; the confident, poised, mature individual; and demonstrated creative, intellectual, and analytical capabilities. Grades are a small part of our selection criteria, although they are important.

In a typical year, how many permanent associates and analysts do you hire? Do you have a summer program for associates or analysts? If so, please describe.

The turnover rate for all employees of J. & W. Seligman & Co. Incorporated is under 10%. Consequently, we have hired no permanent analysts in the past several years.

We have no immediate plans to initiate a summer intern program.

J.P. Morgan & Co.

60 Wall Street
New York, NY 10260
(212) 483-2323

MBA Recruiting Contact(s):
Andrea Beldecos, Vice President,
Corporate Finance Recruiting
Greg Pepe, Associate, Global Markets Recruiting

Company Description

Describe your firm's business and the types of clients served by your finance group(s).

J.P. Morgan provides sophisticated financial services to corporations, governments, financial institutions, private firms, nonprofit institutions, and wealthy individuals throughout the world. Our activities include advising on corporate financial structure; arranging financing in capital and credit markets; underwriting, trading, and investing in an array of currencies and the full range of securities and derivative instruments; serving as investment advisor; and providing select trust, agency, and operational services.

J.P. Morgan advises its clients on the financial implications of corporate strategy and executes transactions when appropriate. These transactions include mergers, acquisitions, divestitures, other forms of corporate restructurings, and privatizations. The firm's global presence and experience are increasingly important to our advisory business as the focus shifts to cross-border transactions.

The firm is an expert on raising money for clients through the full range of instruments—equity and debt underwriting, loan syndications, private placements, and others—in all world markets. We advise clients on their optimal capital structure and implement that advice through transactions in local capital markets or through global offerings.

Morgan is active in the highly liquid debt and equity markets of the established markets, as well as in the markets of the emerging economies. We are a leader and innovator in the derivative business.

All of Morgan's business activities are supported by a strong research capability. In some cases, dedicated research units support specific business areas, such as our Equity Research, which provides sell-side research as part of our U.S. equity sales and distribution function; and Global Research, which provides taxable credit and markets-related research.

Morgan works within the context of a few long-standing and fundamental strategic strengths. We always put our clients' interests first. We take advantage of our deeply rooted and long-standing global network in approaching the needs of our clients. A team approach gives our clients the benefit of the breadth of our capabilities. We operate always with the belief that our reputation for fair dealing is our greatest asset, and we are committed to maintaining the highest standard of conduct.

A matrix of client and product specialists forms the core of J.P. Morgan's Corporate Finance Group. Client specialists are responsible for understanding a client's overall business and financial strategy, as well as for developing an understanding of Morgan's full range of products and services. Product specialists develop expertise in a specific financial area. Corporate Finance professionals counsel clients on and execute the full range of restructuring transactions, including mergers, acquisitions, divestitures, recapitalizations, and privatizations. As the leading international firm doing business in Latin America, Morgan provides advisory services to local governments and businesses. Morgan is extending its expertise to emerging markets elsewhere in the world, including Eastern Europe and the Asia/Pacific region. J.P. Morgan offers a full range of financing options to its clients, including public and privately placed debt and equity securities, syndicated loans, and other credit products in all major world financial markets.

J.P. Morgan's Global Markets group engages in sales and distribution, market making, proprietary risk taking, and investment on a global basis. Morgan has built a well-managed global network of trading locations, supported by decentralized research and a solid infrastructure of communications. The firm makes markets in 15 locations worldwide and takes positions in debt and equity securities, foreign currencies, derivative instruments, government bonds, and developing-country debt. Morgan traders manage risk, liquidity, and interest rate exposure. Morgan has become a strong market leader in the global derivatives business, including swaps, forwards, options and their derivatives, and equity and commodity derivatives, which we use to help clients manage risk as well as for our own account. The firm has focused on building a global sales capability. Sales professionals cover a portfolio of clients based on product/instrument or geography. Research plays a critical role in our markets-related activities, and our research professionals work closely with our traders, sales force, and clients.

The Finance MBA's Job Description

Describe the career path and corresponding responsibilities for an MBA at your firm.

Business units within Corporate Finance and Global Markets employ MBAs. Morgan professionals usually have the opportunity to work in various areas of the firm during the course of their career. This helps them better understand the needs of Morgan's clients and enables them to maximize the firm's abilities to meet these needs.

The first assignment for MBAs hired for Corporate Finance is in Corporate Finance Services (CFS), a group of professionals who work with client and product teams in the marketing, structuring, and execution of financing and advisory assignments. New Associates may be assigned on a rotation to a specific business area or may be handling multiple projects simultaneously. The CFS assignment is followed by an assignment to one of a number of product areas within the Corporate Finance group: Advisory, Emerging Markets–Corporate Finance, or Capital Markets Services. An MBA Associate's career will continue to evolve as the individual develops a broad and solid base of knowledge and experience. The direction of the evolution will be the result of several factors, including an individual's skills and interests, as well as the needs of the firm. Some individuals may have the opportunity to experience an assignment in one of our international offices.

MBAs hired by Global Markets will begin their careers in the positions for which they were hired in one of our market environments. Careers in the Global Markets group are flexible, and after gaining some hands-on experience, an individual may get the opportunity to transfer his or her skills to a new market.

The Recruiting Process

Describe your recruiting process and the criteria by which you select candidates. Are grades a criterion? Is prior experience necessary?

Morgan seeks outstanding creative, analytical, and committed individuals who work well with others and who are willing to assume responsibility. The firm offers hardworking individuals the opportunity to make a significant contribution quickly. Morgan operates with a team approach, which promotes an open discussion of ideas and enables its professionals to learn about parts of Morgan's business outside their own. Members of the firm stress dealing honorably and responsibly with others to maintain the firm's high-quality work environment and high standard of integrity.

Prior experience in the financial services industry is not required or expected for employment. Foreign language skills are considered an asset but are not a requirement.

J.P. Morgan recruits MBAs primarily for positions in New York. The firm also hires MBA students with the right to work overseas for positions in Morgan's offices in Asia, Europe, and Latin America.

J.P. Morgan's Corporate Finance group conducts on-campus interviews for full-time and summer positions. Candidates interested in positions in Global Markets should contact the appropriate recruiter.

Do you have a summer program for associates or analysts? If so, please describe.

J.P. Morgan's extensive program for MBA students during the summer between their first and second years of business school provides a broad exposure to the firm and its businesses. Summer Associates are hired for a general area, based on interests, skills, and past experience, as well as the needs of the firm. Summer Associates have the opportunity to learn about other areas through presentations by Morgan managers and are briefed by senior managers on the firm's business strategy and management philosophy. We also encourage Summer Associates to take the time to meet with officers throughout the firm to identify areas for further exploration. Candidates for the Summer Associate Program should have a serious interest in finance and the financial markets. Most positions are in New York, though opportunities to work abroad may exist for students with the right to work in other jurisdictions. Positions last 10–12 weeks and are scheduled between mid-May and mid-September.

James D. Wolfensohn Incorporated

599 Lexington Avenue
New York, NY 10022
(212) 909-8100
Fax: (212) 909-8161

MBA Recruiting Contact(s):
Carlo Bronzini, Associate

Company Description

Describe your firm's business and the types of clients served by your finance group(s).

James D. Wolfensohn Incorporated (JDWI), an international investment banking firm, advises a select number of corporations and financial institutions. It offers services in three major areas: (1) mergers and acquisitions, including divestitures and strategic alliances, (2) optimizing shareholder value through asset redeployment and balance sheet analysis, and (3) corporate reorganizations, including workouts and bankruptcy.

Its services have been well received in the marketplace. Over the past three years, JDWI has represented clients in transactions worth approximately $25 billion. In the first half of 1993, JDWI was instrumental in three of the year's most important announced merger and acquisition transactions: it represented American Express in the sale of its Shearson unit to Primerica; it represented GPA in its financial arrangements with GECC; and it represented AMAX in the spinoff of its aluminum business and merger of its nonaluminum businesses with Cyprus Minerals.

The firm's investment banking group is exceptionally strong. Clients are served by more than 40 professionals with varied backgrounds in financial analysis, corporate finance, economics, law, and accounting, as well as mergers and acquisitions. JDWI is led by James D. Wolfensohn, who founded the firm in 1981, and Paul A. Volcker, former Chairman of the Federal Reserve System.

JDWI has a strong international focus, with over half of its transactions outside the United States. By way of example, JDWI recently advised the following clients:

- The Hong Kong and Shanghai Banking Corporation Limited in its acquisition of Midland Bank plc

- NCNB Corporation in its acquisition of C&S/Sovran Corporation and its announced acquisition of MNC Financial, Inc.

- Baxter International Inc. in its spin-off of its Caremark Inc. division

- John Labatt Limited in the sale of its JL Foods division to H.J. Heinz Company

- Daimler-Benz AG in its purchase of a stake in Sogeti S.A., parent of Cap Gemini Sogeti S.A., Europe's largest software services company

- E.I. du Pont de Nemours and Company in its sale of half of its coal properties to RWE AG of Germany

International Joint Ventures
JDWI's domestic transactions are enhanced by its international ties. In Asia, the firm works through Fuji-Wolfensohn International. In Europe, JDWI works through J Rothschild Wolfensohn & Co. in London and through the Russian-American Investment Bank in Moscow.

Fuji-Wolfensohn International
The firm has a joint venture with the Fuji Bank to specialize exclusively in Japan-U.S. transactions. The joint venture, Fuji-Wolfensohn International, has seven professionals—four U.S. investment bankers and three experienced Japanese bankers—and can call upon the full range of expertise provided by the JDWI group and by Fuji Bank. Fuji-Wolfensohn International, like JDWI, advises retainer clients on strategic and transaction matters. It has completed a number of transactions, including the investment by Kubota in Cummins Engine, the investment by Ricoh in Gestetner plc, and the purchase of Tri-Gas by Nippon Sanso. Fuji Bank and JDWI have also established an International Advisory Board for Fuji-Wolfensohn in order to further the group's global strategies and the European interests of our clients.

J Rothschild, Wolfensohn & Co.
In March 1992, JDWI formed J Rothschild, Wolfensohn & Co., a joint venture with St. James's Place Capital plc. St. James's Place Capital is the investment holding company for the J Rothschild group, which comprises a range of financial services businesses, including fund management, principal investments and life assurance. The largest shareholder of St. James Place Capital is Lord Roths-Child, one of the world's most eminent financiers.

J. Rothschild, Wolfensohn & Co. provides corporate advisory and investment banking services throughout Western and Eastern Europe to corporations, financial institutions, and government agencies. Mr. Volcker serves on the Board as Chairman, and Mr. Wolfensohn and Lord Rothschild serve as Vice Chairmen.

Russian-American Investment Bank

J Rothschild, Wolfensohn & Co. recently announced its participation, along with American International Group, Chemical Banking Corporation, and Smith Barney, Harris Upham & Co., in cooperation with various Russian investors, in the establishment of a new bank in the Russian Federation. The Russian-American Investment Bank, which has a full banking license, was authorized in a presidential decree signed in Moscow by Russian Federation President Boris Yeltsin. The Investment Bank is a closely held joint stock company organized and domiciled in the Russian Federation with equity investment divided on a fifty-fifty basis between the Russian and Western participants. The Russian shareholders will be the Public Fund for Social Guarantees to Servicemen, the Foreign Trade Bank of Russia, the Pension Fund of Moscow, Gasprom, and the strategic regions of Komi, Tyumen, Kaliningrad, and Yakutia. The Investment Bank's mission will be to assist Russian enterprises in restructuring Russian industry. It will initially concentrate on financial advisory, corporate, and project finance work, with particular emphasis on the natural resources sector and assisting in conversion of the military-industrial infrastructure to civilian purposes. The Investment Bank will also expedite the location of appropriate Russian partners for foreign investors seeking to invest in Russia.

How does your approach to finance differ from that of other firms, and what do you consider to be your strengths and distinctive capabilities?

Several qualities set JDWI apart from other investment banking firms:

- It specializes in long-term, confidential relationships.

- It provides highly sophisticated financial advice and transactional execution.

- It engages in no underwriting or trading for its own account.

- Its dedicated professionals work through a global network with New York headquarters and joint ventures in London and Tokyo.

JDWI finds it is most effective for clients when it works on a long-term strategic basis rather than transaction by transaction. Thus, it has been retained by a number of companies over many years.

The Finance MBA's Job Description

Describe the career path and corresponding responsibilities for an MBA at your firm.

Given JDWI's size and structure, associates can assume significant levels of responsibility early in their careers. During the first years, an associate works as a member of several client teams engaged in specific transactions or analyses. Each client team typically consists of the partner responsible for the client, a senior associate (typically with over five years of experience), an associate (typically with one to five years), and an analyst. As associates gain experience, they take on greater responsibilities within the team, as well as additional client responsibilities. JDWI's philosophy is to develop our professionals as generalist bankers. Associates are therefore given the opportunity to work on assignments across a range of clients and industries in order to gain experience on the strategic and financial issues facing corporations.

Successful associates at JDWI possess a balance of sound analytical abilities and the potential to develop strong client and transaction skills. Due to the size and culture of our firm, our professionals work closely with each other. It is therefore critical for new associates to enjoy working in an extremely interactive and closely-knit environment.

JDWI's basic approach is on-the-job training for associates. However, new associates are also provided with a two-week orientation and training program upon their joining the firm.

The Recruiting Process

Describe your recruiting process and the criteria by which you select candidates. Are grades a criterion? Is prior experience necessary?

JDWI's philosophy is to concentrate hiring at the entry level, seeking each year to attract a small number of MBA candidates with the highest academic standing and greatest potential to become outstanding professionals. New associates have a variety of backgrounds. However, given our focus on investment banking and advisory services, most entering associates typically have some previous experience in corporate finance or M&A.

In a typical year, how many permanent associates and analysts do you hire? Do you have a summer program for associates or analysts? If so, please describe.

JDWI's advisory business has grown at a significant rate over the past several years, and the firm has actively recruited three to four new associates each year.

JDWI plans to hire one or two summer associates each year and considers the summer program a critical component of its full-time recruiting process.

Kidder, Peabody & Co. Incorporated

10 Hanover Square
New York, NY 10005
(212) 510-3000

MBA Recruiting Contact(s):
Linda Bushlow, Vice President,
Investment Banking

Joseph Luciano, Vice President,
Sales, Trading, Research and Asset Management

Michael Burbank, Senior Vice President,
Investment Services (Retail Brokerage)

Company Description

Describe your firm's business and the types of clients served by your finance group(s).

Kidder, Peabody is one of the world's leading investment banking firms, with over 60 offices worldwide. We provide a full complement of investment banking, securities brokerage, and investment advisory services to a diversified group of clients, including corporations, governments, institutional investors, and individual investors.

Principal businesses include securities underwriting, distribution, and trading; restructuring, corporate finance, and mergers and acquisitions; trading of fixed income, equity, and derivative securities; brokerage and research services; asset management; and trading of futures, options, and commodities on a global basis.

Describe your ownership structure.

As a subsidiary of General Electric Capital Services, Kidder, Peabody is committed to integrity, professional excellence, and creativity in the service of its clients. Kidder, Peabody and General Electric have developed a strong relationship, which includes a constant exchange of ideas and business opportunities and has resulted in significant revenues for both parties.

GE has been consistent in its strong support over the last several years. For example, in 1992, an additional $150 million of capital was contributed by GE to help maximize the significant opportunities that were presented in the marketplace. In addition to GE's importance as a client in capital raising and mergers and acquisitions, we have capitalized on joint opportunities with individual GE businesses, including introducing two new mutual funds for investors (Kidder, Peabody Global Equity Fund and Kidder, Peabody Intermediate Fixed Income Fund) in partnership with General Electric Investment Management, or jointly pursuing distressed residential real estate opportunities with General Electric Mortgage Insurance Corporation. We have assisted GE businesses in financing aircraft engines and locomotive and power generation equipment sales, and GE Capital has provided financing assistance to Kidder, Peabody clients.

How does your approach to finance differ from that of other firms, and what do you consider to be your strengths and distinctive capabilities?

To a great extent, Kidder, Peabody's recent success has been due to the fact that the firm was early in recognizing and responding to the major changes in the financial markets that began to emerge in 1989. In essence, Kidder, Peabody recognized that the increasingly complex environment required us to focus our efforts on markets, products and services where we could achieve competitive excellence in serving our clients' specific needs as they arose. The firm embarked on a program to enhance excellence in execution so that its customers can depend on speed and agility in the handling of all transactions.

Although Kidder, Peabody is a full-service firm, we have focused resources on market segments where we can provide a level of value-added service to our clients which is better than, or at least equal to, the best of our competitors in that niche. In Investment Banking, we believe that any one of the large firms is capable of effectively executing the vast majority of capital raising or advisory assignments. While we are committed to providing an execution capability equal to the best on Wall Street, our superior growth is attributable to four features of our approach:

1. We invest in developing a relationship with our clients. Our understanding of the strategic objectives of a company allows us to make a sustained contribution to the achievement of management's goals over the long haul.

2. We focus our efforts on industries in which the combination of our investment banking expertise, research analysis, and sales and trading capability offers our clients superior execution and ideas: natural resources, utilities, environmental services, real estate, health care, transportation, financial services, technology, and retailing, among others.

3. We are willing to tackle our clients' most difficult problems rather than just the run-of-the-mill transactions. This is one reason why, for example, Kidder, Peabody is the market leader in the high-yield private placement market.

4. Our teams cross organizational boundaries to bring all of the capabilities of the firm together to solve client's problems. A good example is the $1 billion of new equity Kidder, Peabody raised for six companies using nontraditional techniques developed by our Equity Division rather than using a traditional public offering approach.

In four years, Kidder, Peabody has gone from being an also-ran in the taxable fixed income business to being one of a handful of major firms with preeminence in several important markets. The strategy has been to build our strength in key areas, one segment at a time, beginning with collateralized mortgage obligations (CMOs) (where Kidder is the premier firm with an 18% market share), moving to residential whole loans, and then to commercial mortgage trading and strategic segments of the Eurobond markets, until an overall leadership position exists as it does today.

Today, Kidder, Peabody is one of the few major firms whose brokerage business is focused solely on the investment needs of the high-net-worth investor, the smaller institution, and the smaller corporation through its Investment Services Division. We have customized our products and services to the unique needs of these three client groups. Small corporations have access to a tailored mix of cash management, pension management, Rule 144, and investment banking services. High-net-worth investors have access to unique portfolio management and reporting services and investment vehicles like the Kidder, Peabody Asset Allocation Fund, developed jointly with Kidder, Peabody Asset Management, or sophisticated derivative-based strategies designed to capitalize on market opportunities. As a result of this focused strategy, our revenue per investment executive is substantially above the industry average. Our experienced national sales force outsells even the largest firms in sophisticated products and is, we believe, the most professional in the industry.

Discuss changes in your firm's revenues (both domestic and international) and professional staff over the past year; over the past five years.

The year 1992 was a record one for Kidder, Peabody, as it was for the securities industry as a whole. With net revenues up 33% to $1.6 billion, our operating profit of over $300 million was double the best year ever.

Like most of our clients, especially those in cyclical industries, performance versus competition is as important as the absolute results. Relative to the other major securities firms in 1992, our net revenue growth of 33% in 1992 exceeded our major competitors for the third year in a row, profits grew faster than our major competitors, and return on equity exceeded our major competitors. Significant market share gains were achieved in numerous areas. Our 7% global underwriting market share ranked us fifth in the world, up from a 5.9% share in 1991 and a threefold increase over our share in 1989. Our international operations were significantly more profitable than a year ago as a result of a well-executed, highly focused strategy.

Each core business made solid contributions to earnings and revenues in 1992. Kidder, Peabody's Investment Banking Group achieved near-record transaction volumes in all major product markets in 1992, with our lead-managed global underwriting market share growing to 7%, up from 5.9% in 1991, and Investment Banking revenues and net income improving significantly over the prior year. The Investment Banking Group employs over 300 professionals worldwide.

Global Sales and Trading posted strong earnings, with significant growth in trading profits in the Fixed Income and Equity businesses. In 1992, the Fixed Income Group ranked fourth in global origination of investment grade debt and was the leading CMO underwriter for the third straight year, with a market share of 18%. This group also has prominent positions in other areas like secondary market trading in Eurobonds, over-the-counter debt options, repo financing and corporate debt, and in trading certain industry groups like environmental services, natural resources and utilities on the equity side. Sales and Trading also maintains a strong position in exchange-traded derivatives. Kidder, Peabody's Equity Group increased market share in technology, environmental, health care, and REIT stocks to levels double or triple past performance. In the primary market, Kidder was involved in managing or comanaging over $6 billion in equity-related transactions.

As for retail brokerage, Kidder, Peabody's Investment Service Division employs 1,200 Investment Executives who offer smart, thoughtful, and personalized investment advice and skillful execution to three select groups—affluent individuals and families, small- to medium-size institutions, and corporations—in 50 major markets in the United States. For the Investment Services Division in 1992, this strategy produced record revenues, effective cost management, and productivity per broker that was the highest of all major Wall Street firms.

During 1992, Kidder, Peabody Asset Management (KPAM) fine-tuned its strategy for the 1990s, which is modeled on a total portfolio approach. As a result, KPAM's assets grew to over $15 billion, a 14% increase over a year earlier.

Kidder, Peabody's Equity Research group includes 46 analysts, and 7 investment strategists in New York, London, and Tokyo, covering 65 industries and more than 650 companies. Analysts and strategists are organized into teams covering broad industry clusters that complement the strengths of Kidder's national sales force, investment banking teams, and sales and trading groups. The Equity Research team provides a full range of research services, including economic, industry, and company research; technical and quantitative analysis; investment policy; and asset allocation recommendations.

The Finance MBA's Job Description

Describe the career path and corresponding responsibilities for an MBA at your firm.

Entry-level associate positions are available for MBAs in various areas of Kidder, Peabody, including Investment Banking, Sales and Trading, Investment Services (retail brokerage), Asset Management, and Equity Research. These departments also hire summer associates between their first and second years of business school. Hiring is done independently by each department.

Describe the opportunities for professional mobility between the various departments in your firm.

Kidder, Peabody is committed to the professional development of its employees. An extensive training program is conducted for all entry-level employees and is designed to introduce the functions of the various departments. Each trainee is treated individually, allowed to advance as rapidly as his or her capabilities warrant, and is compensated accordingly. Our goal is to provide individuals with the support needed for their personal and professional development, and fulfilling this objective many times does result in professional transfers within or across departments in the firm. For example, a regular dialogue is maintained with entry-level associates in Investment Banking, most of whom begin their jobs in a generalist pool. As interests develop, these are discussed, and some individuals choose to specialize in certain departments within Investment Banking as their career develops.

Discuss the lifestyle aspects of a career with your firm (i.e., average hours per week, amount of travel, flexibility to change offices, corporate culture, etc.).

Since success for any financial services firm relies on effective client service, the pace at Kidder, Peabody is swift. The firm's various departments work well together without significant organizational hierarchy, and this factor, combined with the general work pace, makes Kidder, Peabody an extremely exciting place to work.

Kidder, Peabody has an excellent reputation for fostering a collegial work environment. People operate on a first-name basis, project teams tend to be small, and senior members of the team are accessible.

The Recruiting Process

Describe your recruiting process and the criteria by which you select candidates. Are grades a criterion? Is prior experience necessary?

Our recruiting philosophy is to pursue individuals who demonstrate a combination of integrity, intelligence, sales skills, and a strong desire to achieve individual excellence. Creativity, well-developed interpersonal and organizational skills, and a high energy level are critical to an individual's success. While no prior experience is necessary, strong quantitative and qualitative analytical skills combined with a firmly established appreciation for teamwork are important characteristics used to evaluate individuals in the recruiting process.

In a typical year, how many permanent associates and analysts do you hire? Do you have a summer program for associates or analysts? If so, please describe.

Graduating MBAs and summer associates between their first and second years of business school are hired by Investment Banking, Sales and Trading, Investment Services (retail brokerage), Asset Management, and Equity Research. In Investment Banking, approximately 15 permanent associates are hired each year. As for Investment Banking's summer program, Summer Associates spend approximately 12 weeks in an assignment-oriented environment gaining a broad experience and seeing a cross-cut of the division. The Investment Banking Division employed 14 Summer Associates in 1993.

What international opportunities does your firm offer for U.S. citizens? For foreign nationals?

Before the capital markets had become truly global, Kidder, Peabody had already begun to offer its services to clients in the financial capitals of Europe and the Far

East. Kidder, Peabody entered the international marketplace in 1955 with the opening of a London office, followed by expansion into Hong Kong, Geneva, and Tokyo, as well as such international finance centers as Zurich, Paris, Osaka, and Cairo. This global network is strengthened further through alliances with SoPaf/Pasfin, a leading Italian merchant banking group in Milan, and Benito y Monjardin S.V.B., a leading Spanish investment bank and securities firm based in Madrid, and gives Kidder a full-service capability throughout the world.

Career opportunities exist in our international offices, with the Investment Banking and Sales and Trading Groups in London and Tokyo hiring directly as well as soliciting candidates through the New York recruiting process. Candidates for Kidder, Peabody's international offices should have excellent language skills.

Lehman Brothers

American Express Tower
World Financial Center
New York, NY 10285
(212) 298-2000

MBA Recruiting Contact(s):
Rita Haring, Investment Banking
(212) 298-4162
Elisa Fredrickson, Sales and Trading
(212) 298-4488
Christina Deuber, Public Finance
(212) 298-6436

Company Description

Describe your firm's business and the types of clients served by your finance group(s).

Lehman Brothers, one of America's oldest investment banks, is a full-line securities firm serving institutions, governments, institutional, and individual investors in the United States and throughout the rest of the world. Lehman Brothers' business lines include investment and merchant banking, fixed income, equities, commodities and foreign exchange (as well as derivatives of these products), asset management, and financial services (offered through a global network of retail offices).

Lehman Brothers has major operating centers in New York, London, and Tokyo and more than 30 additional offices worldwide.

Describe your ownership structure.

As of December 31, 1992, Lehman Brothers was a division of Shearson Lehman Brothers Inc., a wholly owned subsidiary of Shearson Lehman Brothers Holdings Inc. At that time, American Express owned 100% of the outstanding common stock of Shearson Lehman Brothers Holdings Inc., which represented approximately 92% of Shearson Lehman Brothers Holdings Inc. issued and outstanding voting stock. The remainder was owned by Nippon Life Insurance Company, one of the world's largest life insurance companies.

On March 12, 1993, an agreement was signed with Primerica Corporation and its subsidiary, Smith Barney, Harris Upham & Co., to sell Shearson Lehman Brothers's domestic retail brokerage business (except for such business conducted under the Lehman Brothers name by approximately 500 financial consultants). The proposed transaction is expected to close in the third quarter of 1993. At the close of the transaction, the name of the firm will become Lehman Brothers Inc.

How does your approach to finance differ from that of other firms, and what do you consider to be your strengths and distinctive capabilities?

Lehman Brothers' goal is to build upon the firm's 140-year history of success and to be a leader in all the markets and businesses in which we participate. We will achieve this goal by having the right people in our organization and by adhering to clearly defined objectives and our stated values.

These values are grouped around four major themes:

1. acting as *one firm,*

2. characterized by *teamwork,*

3. with effective and flexible *leadership and management,*

4. making the firm a *world class* organization known for its global presence, profitability, client service, integrity, and superior people.

Lehman Brothers' approach is to work in concert with clients, integrating our efforts with theirs to provide superior service across the investment banking and capital markets businesses. The firm has a long, well-earned reputation for serving its clients and for the professionalism and creativity of its employees. We are continually striving to improve our ability to work as a team, to heighten awareness of client needs, and to deliver still higher levels of service excellence.

Building relationships with clients is the foundation of Lehman Brothers' business philosophy. Toward this end, the firm organizes investment bankers by industry group to enable them to develop expertise in a specific industry, and thus understand and anticipate clients' needs.

The contributions of our people are critical. We maintain a professional atmosphere that fosters cooperation rather than competition without stifling individuality. We place a strong emphasis on teamwork and on leveraging one another's skills, while encouraging each individual's unique creativity and entrepreneurial spirit.

Discuss changes in your firm's revenues (both domestic and international) and professional staff over the past year; over the past five years.

In 1992, Lehman Brothers achieved record financial results, generating revenues of over $2.7 billion, up 17% from 1991. These results clearly reflect the firm's substantial progress since its reorganization under the Lehman Brothers name in 1990. This progress is further evident in the various industry rankings the firm achieved during 1992:

- Lehman Brothers ranked third in managing worldwide equity and debt issues.

- The firm ranked second in lead-managed fixed income securities issued in the United States, with total offerings of $92.6 billion.

- Among managers of U.S. common stock, the firm ranked third for the year. Lehman Brothers' market share more than doubled from 1991 to 30.7%.

- Lehman Brothers is a leader in origination, distribution, and trading of municipal securities. The firm lead-managed nearly $32 billion in tax-exempt securities in 1992.

- Lehman Brothers's Equity and Fixed-Income Research departments were ranked number one in *Institutional Investor* magazine's All-America research poll for 1992.

During 1992, the firm continued to mold the organization and structure of Lehman Brothers according to the firm's stated values. These accomplishments included:

- Implementing a product-based global business development strategy and business group structure that gives clients access to the entire range of the firm's capabilities and talented professionals, without regard to traditional organizational or geographic barriers.

- Strengthening the firm's equities area, creating a customer-driven, highly integrated, global organization.

- Establishing a guaranteed investment contract subsidiary rated AAA by the major ratings agencies.

- Developing an integrated derivative products unit within the fixed income, equity, foreign exchange, and commodities business groups that better meets the complex global needs of clients.

- Upgrading the firm's foreign exchange effort to strengthen the unit's links with fixed income, equities, derivative products, and investment banking businesses.

- Continuing to strengthen the firm's international capabilities by integrating and developing the worldwide expertise and coverage necessary to serve the needs of clients. In addition to global institutional coverage, the firm is upgrading its asset management capabilities and multiproduct offerings to midsize institutions and high-net-worth individuals.

In pursuit of the goals of superior client service and employee development, all organizational and management changes have been aimed at facilitating cooperation and responsiveness; all compensation and advancement standards have been linked to teamwork and client satisfaction. At the top of this system is the firm's partnership structure, dedicated to continuity and investment in a shared enterprise. The driving principle behind these actions is the belief that the firm succeeds only when its various businesses work together.

The Finance MBA's Job Description

Describe the career path and corresponding responsibilities for an MBA at your firm.

Lehman Brothers prides itself on the variety of backgrounds and range of achievements represented by its professionals. Before joining the firm, many Lehman Brothers professionals had careers in areas such as law, medicine, public service, and private industry, as well as in finance. This diversity instills creativity in and provides depth to the firm.

Lehman Brothers is committed to developing well-rounded professionals and encourages Associates to take on as much responsibility as they can handle. Each Associate is given the opportunity to build a broad base of skills, and the firm constantly monitors each Associate's development, working with him or her to help achieve specific career goals.

To prepare incoming Associates for these exciting and challenging opportunities, Lehman Brothers offers well-structured training programs that strongly reflect the firm's values. Investment Banking, Sales and Trading, and Public Finance Associates share in joint classroom training, team-building activities, and social events as part of the "one firm" concept. Functional business knowledge is covered in the following programs.

For incoming Investment Banking Associates, classroom training during the first month enables them to hone their skills in accounting and finance while learning the analytical tools they will use throughout their careers. This training is followed by several month-long rotations in different industry and product groups.

These short rotations are followed by five-month assignments during which Associates gain hands-on experience in industries or product groups of particular interest to them and participate as fully contributing members of project teams with bankers of all levels.

Associates may then decide to continue with the same group or move on to other areas. Lehman Brothers works to maintain the flexibility that allows Associates many opportunities to change their specializations or focuses as their careers progress.

Classroom training for Sales and Trading Associates is followed by two rounds of rotations—the first providing Associates with general exposure to a variety of product areas, the second allowing each Associate to concentrate on specific areas of interest.

Each Associate is assigned to work with a senior professional who provides guidance during the early stages of the Associate's career. Through this apprenticeship process, Trading Associates gradually assume responsibility for individual profit and loss centers, and Sales Associates develop their own account relationships.

Public Finance Associates serve as generalists during most of their first year, working with a variety of municipal clients. After the generalist training program, each Associate joins either a specialty or regional group.

The Recruiting Process

Describe your recruiting process and the criteria by which you select candidates. Are grades a criterion? Is prior experience necessary?

In our recruiting efforts we look for individuals who possess a keen intellect, a powerful desire to succeed, and the resourcefulness to produce results. Because of the emphasis on teamwork, we also want people who can cooperate and leverage one another's skills while encouraging each individual's unique creativity and entrepreneurial spirit.

Do you have a summer program for associates or analysts? If so, please describe.

Lehman Brothers' Summer Associate Program provides students at the midpoint of their graduate school education an opportunity to evaluate the working environment and career opportunities at the firm.

Investment Banking and Public Finance Summer Associates work as full members of client teams on a variety of transactions. They also enjoy extensive contact with Lehman Brothers professionals at all levels through discussion groups, seminars, and informal social functions.

Sales and Trading Summer Associates are assigned to a ten-week placement in an individual business unit, although they spend one day of each week in a different product area, covering a variety of businesses over the course of the summer. In addition, they attend lectures by senior professionals and participate in weekly market update sessions.

Merrill Lynch & Co. Inc.

World Financial Center
250 Vesey Street
New York, NY 10281-1331
(212) 449-9836

MBA Recruiting Contact(s):
John W. Rae, Jr.
Director, Recruiting and Training

Company Description

Describe your firm's business and the types of clients served.

Merrill Lynch is a global investment banking firm, headquartered in New York with a presence in 29 countries worldwide. It is the leading underwriting and brokerage firm in the United States.

Merrill Lynch acts as principal, agent, underwriter, market maker, broker, and financial advisor to its clients. The firm is fundamentally client driven, bringing together issuers and investors.

Our institutional businesses—Investment Banking, and Debt and Equity Markets—offer an expansive range of services to 6,000 corporate, institutional, and governmental clients worldwide. These groups are based in New York with major offices in London, Tokyo, and Hong Kong and representation in other major financial centers. Our individual investor business—Private Client—provides investment, banking, credit, money management, and insurance products and services to 7 million individuals and small businesses worldwide. These groups are headquartered in Princeton, NJ.

In a little over a decade, the firm has built a premier institutional franchise with clients on a worldwide basis. Since 1988, Merrill Lynch has been the leading global underwriter of debt and equity securities. Two major trends are creating new opportunities for the firm globally: the spread of capitalism and an increasing variety of financing alternatives. In Latin America, Eastern Europe, and the Asia-Pacific Rim, we expect growth to outpace that of more developed regions.

Describe your ownership structure.

Merrill Lynch & Co. is a publicly owned corporation, trading on the principal stock exchanges in New York,

London, Toronto, Paris, and Tokyo. Stockholders' equity at December 25, 1992, totaled $4.6 billion, with 103.6 million shares outstanding.

Merrill Lynch was the first member firm of the New York Stock Exchange to go public in June 1971, and a month later it became the first member firm whose own stock was traded on the Big Board. Previously it had been a partnership.

How does your approach to finance differ from that of other firms, and what do you consider to be your strengths and distinctive capabilities?

The strength of our organization is based on leadership in both the institutional and retail sectors. Merrill Lynch's ability to capitalize on the synergies that exist between these sectors—specifically, a strong distribution function complementing an origination and trading capability—distinguishes its strategy from that of its competitors. With the largest distribution capabilities on Wall Street and an integrated global network, the firm has the unique ability to place deals and facilitate transactions worldwide.

Discuss changes in your firm's revenues (both domestic and international) and professional staff over the past year; over the past five years.

The year 1992 was Merrill Lynch's second straight year of record profits. Net earnings to common shareholders were the highest ever achieved by a U.S. public securities firm ($894 million). Shareholders' equity rose 20% to $4.6 billion, the highest of any U.S. securities company. The firm's return on average common equity was 22%. Merrill Lynch earned more than $1.6 billion in 1992—up more than 57% from the strong showing the previous year. The firm employs 40,100 people worldwide, down from 50,000 in 1987.

The Finance MBA's Job Description

Describe the career path and corresponding responsibilities for an MBA at your firm.

Merrill Lynch invests substantial resources in identifying and recruiting superior candidates. In 1992–1993 the firm hired 106 MBAs: 46 in Investment Banking, 46 in Debt & Equity Markets, 6 in Public Finance, 5 in Treasury & Finance, 1 in Securities Research, and 2 in the Individual Investor Group.

The following three businesses recruit the most MBAs:

- Investment Banking is responsible for corporate and institutional client relationships worldwide. Through the delivery of advisory services and financial products, the division focuses on the needs of issuer clients. Included in this division are mergers and acquisitions, leveraged buyout fund management, real estate, project financing, relationship management, and several specialty functions.

- Debt Markets offers issuing and investing clients a complete array of debt financing alternatives in short-, medium-, and long-term debt products. The division is integrated vertically to include origination, trading, fixed income, marketing, research, and new product development. Major product areas are money markets, global debt financing, mortgage capital, financial futures and options, U.S. governments and agencies, foreign exchange, and municipal markets.

- Equity Markets is structured to provide institutional investor clients with origination, trading, syndication, and wholesale services worldwide. The division also works with investment banking in serving corporate and government issuers.

Career paths and corresponding responsibilities vary depending on the business division. An MBA joining Investment Banking, for example, typically enters as an associate, responsible for the details of executing transactions and preparing proposals. After approximately four years, associates are eligible for promotion to vice president. Vice presidents manage the execution of transactions and identify new opportunities with clients. About three years later, vice presidents become eligible for promotion to director, or the more senior title of managing director. Directors and managing directors are responsible for maintenance of client relationships and identification of new business opportunities.

New associates generally join the firm in early August and complete a five-week firm-wide development program. Besides serving as an orientation to Merrill Lynch, the program builds strong ties among the participants. The academic component includes team assignments, case studies, simulations, and hands-on interaction with trading games.

Describe the opportunities for professional mobility between the various departments in your firm.

New associates work in a specific department, though they have much contact throughout the firm. As their interests change and as our businesses evolve, new opportunities are often available firmwide.

Discuss the lifestyle aspects of a career with your firm (i.e., average hours per week, amount of travel, flexibility to change offices, corporate culture, etc.).

Lifestyles vary depending on which business unit an MBA joins. Requirements for each division are typical for the financial services industry.

The Recruiting Process

Describe your recruiting process and the criteria by which you select candidates. Are grades a criterion? Is prior experience necessary?

Merrill Lynch participates in on-campus presentations and events, and on-campus interviews. Successful candidates are called back for final interviews in New York. The firm adheres to school policies in its recruiting practices.

We seek individuals with a record of achievement and excellence. Successful candidates have strong analytical skills and an understanding of strategic issues. They communicate effectively, think creatively, work well with others, and act decisively. Academic performance and prior work experience are also important criteria, though prior work in the industry is not necessary.

In a typical year, how many permanent associates and analysts do you hire? Do you have a summer program for associates and analysts? If so, please describe.

Hiring is based on the needs of each business division, and recruiting goals are set early in the fall for the coming recruiting season. In 1993, we hired 106 MBAs.

Most business divisions of the firm participate in the summer associate program. Summer associates have significant responsibilities and are involved with a variety of transactions. Scheduled activities and seminars with senior management offer summer associates frequent exposure and the opportunity to expand their knowledge of the firm. In 1993, 98 summer associates were hired across the firm.

Montgomery Securities

600 Montgomery Street
San Francisco, CA 94111
(415) 627-2000

MBA Recruiting Contact(s):
Sharon Henning, Vice President
(415) 627-2793

Company Description

Describe your firm's business and the types of clients served by your finance group(s).

Montgomery Securities is a San Francisco–based investment bank with a national and international presence. Privately held, Montgomery Securities is the nation's premier equity-focused broker/dealer specializing in emerging-growth companies. In 1992, the firm managed over $9 billion in public and private offerings and merger and acquisition transactions and traded over 1.6 billion shares on the listed and over-the-counter markets, ranking sixteenth. Montgomery's investment banking activities are conducted through four departments: Corporate Finance, which includes underwritings, mergers and acquisitions, and private placements; Research; Sales; and Trading. In addition, Montgomery's investment management business, with assets of over $3 billion, manages a family of mutual funds and handles the money management needs of corporations and high-net-worth individuals. In 1993, the firm established a fixed income effort, which will focus on private placement and public debt financings for its growing client base.

The activities of each of the firm's departments are closely coordinated and are focused on four industries: technology, consumer, health care, and financial services. Montgomery's investment banking clients consist of emerging- and established-growth companies located throughout the United States. The firm's institutional brokerage clients include over 1,100 institutions worldwide. A description of the firm's departments follows.

Corporate Finance
The Corporate Finance Department initiates, develops, and maintains relationships with the premier emerging-growth companies in each of the industry groups Montgomery focuses on. Corporate finance professionals have extensive experience in analyzing and identifying a company's financing requirements and in executing transactions, including public and private equity offerings, mergers and acquisitions, and public and private debt. The department is staffed with over 60 professionals whose skills combine specific industry experience and investment banking expertise. The department is organized along industry lines to take advantage of the firm's research and trading strengths in technology, consumer services, health care, and financial services.

Research Department
The foundation for Montgomery's success in serving both its corporate finance clients and its institutional brokerage customers is its strong Research Department. The department is staffed with over 40 Senior Analysts and Analyst Associates whose skills combine industry-specific focus and expertise covering large and small capitalization companies. Montgomery covers 350 companies, including 190 noninvestment banking clients. The department is organized along industry groups—technology, consumer services, health care, and financial services—and its primary goal is superior performance for Montgomery clients.

Sales Department
Montgomery Securities' effectiveness as an underwriter owes much to the strength and reputation of its Institutional Sales Department. This reputation has been built over two decades through relationships with clients that are based on trust, knowledge of the markets, past money-making performance, and superior service. Montgomery's institutional sales force covers more than 1,100 domestic and international institutions.

In 1992, the Private Client Department of Montgomery Securities was established in keeping with the corporate philosophy of providing focused attention to an exclusive universe of clients. Just as our firm has focused on the largest and most influential financial institutions and the most substantial and fastest growing corporations, Montgomery Securities has now built a private investor business based on exclusively servicing the investment needs of wealthy individuals and their families.

Trading Department
The Trading Department, one of the largest outside New York, complements and enhances the Corporate Finance, Research, and Sales departments. Montgomery is a major market maker in common stocks traded in the over-the-counter market. In addition, Montgomery is very active in the trading of blocks of common stock of companies listed on the New York Stock Exchange and other national securities exchanges. Our trading focus is in the stocks of companies that are actively covered by the

Research Department. These activities provide the after-market trading support that is essential in ensuring a successful public offering and maintaining an efficient market for a company's stock.

Fixed Income Department

As the firm's client base continued to expand and its clients continued to grow, Montgomery made a strategic decision to enter the fixed income market in 1993. It is the intention of the firm to develop highly competitive private and public debt financing capabilities. The group is initially focusing on public and private new issues.

Describe your ownership structure.

Montgomery Securities is a privately held general partnership.

How does your approach to finance differ from that of other firms, and what do you consider to be your strengths and distinctive capabilities?

Montgomery Securities differentiates itself through an integrated, focused approach that offers selected investment banking services to emerging- and established-growth companies. The firm's investment banking relationships, quality research, and trading capabilities, coupled with an industry-focused orientation, allow Montgomery professionals to become experts in specific sectors. The close communication among the firm's corporate finance personnel, research analysts, and sales force gives Montgomery a unique ability to communicate a client company's story to institutional investors effectively and to distribute that company's securities efficiently. This is made possible by Montgomery's small size and single location, together with the firm's acknowledged expertise in the companies and industries it follows. Montgomery's after-market support for its corporate finance clients, including ongoing research coverage, institutional road shows, investment conferences, corporate finance advice, and trading of the clients' stock, is superior and again reflects Montgomery's focused approach, close communications, and industry expertise. This focused market strategy differentiates Montgomery from the larger New York-based investment banks and is the primary reason for Montgomery's tremendous growth and profitability in its 24-year history.

The Finance MBA's Job Description

Describe the career path and corresponding responsibilities for an MBA at your firm.

In the Corporate Finance Department, an MBA begins her or his career as a generalist Associate before specializing in one of Montgomery's four business sectors. Montgomery's client teams are traditionally lean, so an Associate is ensured significant client contact and responsibility from the beginning. An Associate's responsibilities focus primarily on analyzing, structuring, and executing transactions, as well as assisting in new business development. The levels above Associate are (in order) Vice President, Principal, and Managing Director (Partner). Advancement and success are contingent on personal performance. As an individual advances, that individual's responsibilities for clients and new business development increase.

Upon the completion of a comprehensive training program in the Private Client Department, Associates help facilitate long-term investment relationships with wealthy individuals and family groups. Interacting closely with the research and trading departments, Associates will provide a portfolio approach for private clients' investment needs. Associates will be trained as product generalists, knowledgeable in all markets and supported by a network of specialists in each. The Associate Program offers individuals a unique entrepreneurial experience with compensation tied directly to one's efforts.

In the Research Department, entry-level Associates are assigned to work directly with Research Analysts and may come in on many different levels, depending on prior knowledge and experience. Working with the Analyst, the Associate develops her or his expertise researching industries and analyzing companies, with the goal of being promoted to an Analyst with a specific industry and company focus.

Entry-level MBAs joining the Trading Department begin their career at Montgomery as junior traders with the goal of being promoted to a Senior Trader with their own group of stocks.

Discuss the lifestyle aspects of a career with your firm (i.e., average hours per week, amount of travel, flexibility to change offices, corporate culture, etc.).

A career in investment banking at Montgomery is exciting and rewarding and requires a significant commitment of time and energy. The hours can be long and the travel extensive. Montgomery is, however, located in San Francisco, and this location reflects a commitment to a lifestyle outside the office. The hours worked and the extent of travel vary depending on an individual's work load.

The Recruiting Process

Describe your recruiting process and the criteria by which you select candidates. Are grades a criterion? Is prior experience necessary?

Because of its size and corporate philosophy, Montgomery offers an unstructured investment banking environment. Montgomery is seeking bright, hard-working, personable candidates who are self-motivated. Strong analytical and communication skills, as well as creativity and initiative, are important. Prior investment banking experience is definitely helpful but not always necessary. Advancement and success are contingent upon personal performance.

In a typical year, how many permanent associates and analysts do you hire? Do you have a summer program for associates or analysts? If so, please describe.

In 1994 the firm expects to hire 15–20 entry-level MBAs. Montgomery does not offer a summer program for MBAs.

Morgan Stanley & Co. Incorporated

1251 Avenue of the Americas
New York, NY 10020
(212) 703-8482

MBA Recruiting Contact(s):
Patricia Palumbo

Company Description

Describe your firm's business and the types of clients served by your finance group(s).

The Investment Banking Division consists of four closely related business units: Corporate Finance, Financing and Advisory Services, Morgan Stanley Realty, and Capital Market Services.

Corporate Finance
Corporate Finance is responsible for initiating, developing, and maintaining the firm's investment banking relationships with clients worldwide; for providing financial advice; and, in partnership with other specialized areas of the firm, for executing specific client transactions.

The Corporate Finance Department is organized into teams of regional and industry specialists. The regional coverage groups provide a strong Morgan Stanley presence in the United States, Canada, Western and Eastern Europe, Latin America, the Middle East, the Far East, and Australia. The industry groups provide special expertise in the following sectors: commercial banking, financial entrepreneurs, food and consumer products, health care, insurance, media, natural resources, public utilities, retail, technology, telecommunications, and transportation. In addition, we have a commitment to advise government and private sector clients on the privatization of state-owned enterprises.

Financing and Advisory Services
The Financing and Advisory Services Department is a confederation of those groups having responsibility for the execution of most investment banking transactions for our clients. Financing and Advisory Services consists of Mergers and Acquisitions, Financing Services, Private Investment (known as Princes Gate), and the newly created Project Finance Group.

 All junior Associates joining the firm begin their careers in the Financing and Advisory Services Department.

Mergers and Acquisitions. Morgan Stanley is one of a small number of investment banking firms consistently identified as a leader in domestic and international mergers and acquisitions. Mergers and Acquisitions (M&A) provides corporate and financial clients with a wide range of financial advisory services in situations involving mergers, acquisitions, defenses, proxy contests, divestitures, spin-offs, joint ventures, and restructurings.

Many of our M&A assignments involve complex, competitive situations that require a high degree of creativity, analytical skill, and judgment. M&A professionals must be proficient in a wide range of technical skills (e.g., legal, tax, and accounting expertise) and understand an extensive number of strategic alternatives in the context of any particular transaction. In addition, individuals may develop specialized expertise in one or several of a wide variety of industries, including communications, natural resources, financial institutions, health care, and technology, where complex regulatory, financial, and business knowledge can add considerable value toward meeting the strategic objectives of our clients.

Financing Services. The Financing Services Group (FSG) is responsible for the execution of all equity offerings (initial public offerings, reverse leveraged buyout and recapitalizations, convertible securities, derivative securities, common stock, and warrants), complex debt issuances, and other capital markets-related business. Among other things, Financing Services professionals have responsibility for the business investigation and due diligence process, registration statement and prospectus drafting, documentation, development of the road show presentation and schedule, and negotiation of the terms under which the firm will underwrite a company's securities.

Private Investment. The Private Investment Department manages an investment partnership, Princes Gate Investors, L.P. This partnership was established in 1992 to invest globally in special situations, and it consists of capital commitments totaling approximately $450 million. The purpose of the partnership is to seek out investment opportunities generally in the form of minority equity positions, of short to medium term in duration.

Project Finance. Based in London, this group works in close coordination with other areas of the firm, such as Corporate Finance and Capital Markets, to structure discrete financing for major capital projects around the world.

Morgan Stanley Realty

Morgan Stanley Realty (MSR), an integrated department within the Investment Banking Division, is responsible for providing real estate services for Morgan Stanley's corporate clients, as well as for major owners and developers of real estate. As a principal, MSR invests in real estate through the Morgan Stanley Real Estate Fund, L.P. (MSREF), with more than $800 million of committed capital. MSREF is focused on high-yield real estate investments that utilize MSR's creativity in structuring acquisitions and selecting venture partners. Morgan Stanley has the oldest established real estate franchise on Wall Street, with over 60 years of experience.

Capital Market Services

Capital Market Services—responsible for structuring, pricing, and managing public offerings and private placements of debt and equity securities—provides a link between Investment Banking and Equity and Fixed Income Division of the firm. This area is composed of Debt Capital Markets and Equity Capital Markets.

Debt Capital Markets. Debt Capital Markets is responsible for the solicitation and execution of Morgan Stanley's primary debt and related products business. The group consists of Syndicate, Continuously Offered Products, Market Coverage, High Yield, Private Placements, and Preferred Stock. Together these groups provide a sophisticated global capital markets service, including product development, marketing, and execution, from Morgan Stanley offices in New York, London, Tokyo, Frankfurt, and Zurich.

Debt Syndicate is broadly responsible for developing and implementing the firm's strategy for the global underwriting business. On a day-to-day basis, Syndicate manages the worldwide distribution of public offerings of securities for Morgan Stanley's clients. Typically, this involves engaging in competitive and negotiated transactions, as well as providing judgments with respect to the optimal structure for a particular security, the timing of entering the market, the composition of the underwriting syndicate, and the pricing of the issue. The pricing process requires assessing the market risk for a given credit and structure and committing the firm's capital to ensure the successful execution of the transaction. Specific focus is given to obtaining the best possible pricing for the client. In managing the distribution of securities, Syndicate is also responsible for hedging Morgan Stanley's liability until syndicate restrictions are terminated.

The Continuously Offered Products area, a subgroup of Debt Syndicate, assists clients in establishing commercial paper and medium-term note (MTN) programs in the United States and Europe. Morgan Stanley acts as either principal or agent in the distribution of these securities through the firm's global fixed income sales network.

The role of the Market Coverage Group is to advise Morgan Stanley's investment banking clients on financing strategies in the global capital markets. Market Coverage professionals maintain a regular dialogue with their clients on topics such as new product ideas, financing alternatives, and general developments in the debt, swap, and preferred stock markets worldwide.

Private Placements is responsible for coordinating the origination, structuring, execution, and distribution of private debt transactions for U.S. and foreign issuers. Preferred Stock is responsible for structuring and executing public and private straight (i.e. nonconvertible) fixed- and floating-rate preferred stock. Preferred stocks, although equity from a tax perspective, have investment characteristics similar to those of fixed income securities and are sold primarily through the Firm's Fixed Income Division.

Equity Capital Markets. Equity Capital Markets has global product responsibility for corporate equity-related transactions, including common stock, initial public offerings, subsidiary initial public offerings, convertibles, warrants, and share repurchases in the domestic and global markets. The specific functions of the group include:

- *Product management.* Serving as a knowledge base for the valuation, trading, and issuance of equity securities.

- *Syndicate.* Managing and pricing new equity issues.

- *Business development.* Assisting Market Coverage and the Corporate Finance coverage groups in marketing Morgan Stanley's equity capabilities to corporate clients.

- *Product development.* Developing new equity securities, in both domestic and international markets, that meet the needs of corporate clients and institutional equity investors.

- *Strategic advice.* Assisting Corporate Finance coverage professionals and Mergers and Acquisitions in structuring equity securities and in determining the effect of financial policy decisions on equity values.

Morgan Stanley is a leading underwriter of equity and equity-related securities. In 1992, the firm was managing underwriter for 174 equity and equity-related financing, totaling approximately $45 billion.

The Finance MBA's Job Description

Describe the career path and corresponding responsibilities for an MBA at your firm.

All Associates hired in investment banking spend their first two years working on a variety of transactions with team leaders from the Financing and Advisory Services Department, the Corporate Finance Department, Capital Market Services, and Real Estate. There is a mix of assignments and opportunities provided each Associate, ranging from transaction execution to business development initiatives, to rotations in highly specialized areas in various departments. It is our philosophy with regard to the investment banking business that it must be managed on a long-term basis, and therefore that we emphasize the importance of training and career development of our junior professionals. Thus, Junior Associates are provided the opportunity to develop broad-based execution skills. At the same time, through specific client coverage designations, Associates have the opportunity to establish and cultivate personal relationships with our most important clients.

Describe the opportunities for professional mobility between the various departments in your firm.

Morgan Stanley's primary objective is to develop investment bankers who have broad knowledge of and experience in the investment banking field. Over the course of one's career, an individual should expect to work in several different areas of the Investment Banking Division. The initial two years in the Financing and Advisory Services Department is the first stage in the ongoing process of training and development of broad-based investment banking skills.

In staffing a new assignment, managers consider which professionals have not worked on similar assignments and would benefit from doing so. An integral part of the staffing process is the Assignments Associate, whose primary responsibility is to manage the staffing of projects and, in so doing, to ensure that professionals obtain the support they need and gain exposure to a broad range of projects and clients.

All assignments are executed by teams, which typically consist of two to four professionals and may include a Managing Director, a Principal or a Vice President, an Associate, and an Analyst. (Analysts are college graduates who typically intend to go to business school after working two to three years at Morgan Stanley.) All professionals are on several teams concurrently, two to four of which may be active at the same time. Team assignments may last from a few days to several months, and the team structure allows Associates to work with various Managing Directors and other officers.

Such diversity in the types of projects assigned and in the people with whom one works enables Associates to obtain excellent training in and exposure to all aspects of investment banking. This environment, however, forces Associates to learn how to manage the demands of various assignments that are active simultaneously. The firm places a premium on an Associate's ability to assume the responsibility for as much of the work load as possible.

An important element of the career development process is the evaluation and discussion of individual performance at the conclusion of each significant assignment. This feedback process plays a critical role in identifying each individual's major strengths and longer-term career goals. In addition, a more formal evaluation of an Associate's overall performance occurs at least twice a year. At this time, senior investment banking officers and department managers who have had extensive working relationships with the individual review the person's contributions and development. The review is quite specific, detailing areas to be worked on so that the individual can continue his or her development as a successful investment banker.

Discuss the lifestyle aspects of a career with your firm (i.e., average hours per week, amount of travel, flexibility to change offices, corporate culture, etc.).

The professionals at Morgan Stanley have always exhibited a high level of personal flexibility, professional expertise, and dedication. In turn, they have enjoyed a high degree of opportunity and challenge. The emphasis placed on teamwork and mutual support at the firm has contributed to a positive working environment where meeting clients' needs through the team approach is the main objective. Standards for compensation, advancement, and promotion are based exclusively on merit.

What international opportunities does your firm offer for U.S. citizens? For foreign nationals?

Each major business unit is managed on both a worldwide and local basis. The firm maintains international offices in London, Tokyo, Madrid, Singapore, Seoul, Frankfurt, Milan, Hong Kong, Melbourne, Paris, Toronto, and Zurich. Investment banking professionals in these offices and in New York are responsible for marketing the firm's products and services to clients and prospective clients outside the United States.

As the firm's overseas offices have grown, there has been an increasing focus on hiring foreign nationals possessing cultural sensitivity and the willingness to make a long-term commitment to a particular office. Virtually all of the Associates destined for foreign offices will spend time training in New York during early phases of their careers.

NationsBank

NationsBank Corporate Center, NC1-007-2108
Charlotte, NC 28255
(704) 386-8200

MBA Recruiting Contact(s):
Mark Brown, Manager, College Recruiting

Company Description

Describe your firm's business and the types of clients served by your finance group(s).

Our name is one of the newest among U.S. banking giants, but our competitive presence among the nation's most influential financial institutions has been well known for decades. NationsBank is one of the largest banking companies in the nation, with more than 1700 banking offices in nine states and the District of Columbia.

We have achieved this status through aggressive, disciplined growth. We maintain a corporate culture that values teamwork and loyalty in a workplace where people genuinely care for one another and are committed to serving their clients effectively. Our vision is relatively straightforward: We seek to be the premier provider of financial services within the geographic franchise of NationsBank and to be a significant provider of financial services and products to clients nationwide.

One of the areas in which we strive to be the best is in our Institutional Bank. The Institutional Bank targets corporations and institutions with sales in excess of $100 million plus selected industry groups. It is composed of our Corporate Bank, which includes Lending, International, Treasury Management, and Specialized Industry Groups; our Investment Bank, which houses our Products and Structuring groups, both domestic and international; and Global Sales and Trading, which includes our Institutional Securities and Foreign Exchange Trading business. The Institutional Bank is composed of some 2100 people located in 17 cities in the United States and abroad.

Clients within the Institutional Bank have financing needs that go far beyond traditional bank products. Meeting those needs is the essence of our business. It requires a highly coordinated and focused effort among our lenders, product specialists, and securities people. This is best done by a rather centralized structure where all of our people are in constant touch with new trends and developments, and knowledge and skills are therefore more easily shared and focused on the customer.

The Finance MBA's Job Description

Describe the career path and corresponding responsibilities for an MBA at your firm.

We are broadening the traditional role of our Corporate Relationship Manager, who in the past has principally focused on lending, to include the responsibilities of a financial advisor. This is done through the Corporate Bank Associate Program, which is designed to develop financial, analytical, and sales skills in preparation for a position as a Corporate Relationship Manager dealing with multi-billion-dollar national and international companies.

Training begins with six weeks of classroom instruction in Charlotte or Dallas. You will then put your skills to work in our Credit Department. During this core training phase, you will work directly with Corporate Relationship Managers in a variety of areas. After 9–12 months in the Credit Department, having further developed your financial, analytical, and communication skills, you will return to the classroom for the Relationship Manager Development Program (RMDP). These final four weeks of training will focus on NationsBank's Corporate Products, as well as on sales and negotiating skills.

Upon successful completion of training, you will spend 12 months in the Corporate Bank as an Associate and a member of a lending team. You will then spend 12–18 months in our Institutional Bank. This time will be spent in rotations through two or three of its product specialty areas, such as Structured Finance, Sales and Syndication, Capital Markets, or Mergers and Acquisitions. Time will also be spent on the funds floor through Global Trading and Distribution. Upon completion of your assignment in the Institutional Bank, you will be placed into the Corporate Bank in one of our major metropolitan markets: New York, Chicago, Los Angeles, Atlanta, Charlotte, Houston, Dallas, Richmond, Tampa, Miami, and Nashville.

The Recruiting Process

Describe your recruiting process and the criteria by which you select candidates. Are grades a criterion? Is prior experience necessary?

We are looking for MBAs who are interested in a career in sales, sophisticated financial analysis, and a competitive transactions-oriented environment. Strong analytical, communication, and sales skills are required along with the willingness to relocate. Work experience is strongly preferred.

Nomura Securities International, Inc.

2 World Financial Center
Building B
New York, NY 10281

MBA Recruiting Contact(s):
Ariel Kochi, Vice President
(212) 667-9237
Fax: (212) 667-1016

Company Description

Describe your firm's business and the types of clients served by your finance group(s).

Nomura Securities International, Inc. (NSI) is a wholly owned subsidiary of the Nomura Securities Co., Ltd. (Nomura), the world's largest securities firm. With shareholder equity exceeding $14 billion and total assets of more than $23.2 billion, Nomura is the most profitable financial institution in the world.

A medium-size investment banking company, NSI employs more than 800 people in the United States. NSI has evolved from a company handling primarily Japanese-related securities into a full-fledged member of the American financial community and also is a member of the major securities and commodities exchanges, as well as a primary dealer in U.S. Treasury securities. U.S. operations, which began in 1927, have expanded to include two branch offices in Chicago and one in Los Angeles. Today, NSI offers a wide range of products and services: sales, trading, investment banking, mutual funds, and portfolio and asset management.

NSI is continually in a state of evolution as the firm works to develop new businesses, such as the high-yield and Latin American departments. Two years ago, 80% of NSI's investment banking revenues were due to Japanese-related business (country funds distributed in Japan, Tokyo Stock Exchange listing fees, etc.). This past year over 40% of revenues were from non-Japan-related business (Compania Cervecerias Unidas S.A., Chic by H.I.S., and JAFCO II). Our investment banking group was active with numerous initial public offerings and private placements and created innovative financing structures such as ROSA II and Ivory.

In addition to its financial strength and the breadth of its capabilities, Nomura is internationally renowned for its innovation in finance:

- Nomura introduced and popularized the Gensaki, a Japanese bond sale and repurchase agreement that has developed into an important short-term investment instrument.

- Nomura pioneered the expansion of the Japanese financial community by introducing foreign companies to the country's rapidly growing capital markets. The firm designs and implements investor relations programs for client companies and arranges the listing of their shares on the Tokyo Stock Exchange. In the past, Nomura has listed Anheuser-Busch, AT&T, General Electric, Kraft, and J.P. Morgan, among others.

- With the increase in global investing, more and more institutional and individual investors rely on Nomura's international research, sales, and trading capabilities. Nomura's leadership position in the Japanese market as a broker/dealer and market maker provides an unparalleled resource for investors.

- Working to meet clients' needs, Nomura has established relationships with financial institutions to help ensure the development of innovative products in the areas of leveraged leasing, project financing, real estate investing within the United States, and mergers and acquisitions.

- NSI's Equity Derivatives group is constantly at the top of the New York Stock Exchange chart of 15 most active firms in program trading volume.

The growing importance of investment management has led NSI to form additional companies to provide service to clients. Nomura Corporate Research and Asset Management (NCRAM) is a money management firm with a worldwide client base specializing in high-yield bond investments. Combining the credit expertise of NCRAM with Nomura's tremendous capital base and global distribution capability has helped the firm to achieve a preeminent position in asset management. Expertise in corporate credit also provides the foundation for our aggressive worldwide expansion into proprietary trading, structured finance, and other related merchant and investment banking activities.

With our mortgage-backed securities business continuing to grow, Nomura created a subsidiary, Nomura Asset Capital Corporation (NACC), to conduct our real estate and nonagency trading and financing. NACC, though initially focusing on commercial mortgages, will transact in the commercial and residential loan markets, as well as the asset-backed securities market.

Emphasizing an empirical, problem-solving approach to its studies, Nomura Research Institutes conducts fundamental research on a wide range of socioeconomic and socioscientific issues, as well as on matters of long-term relevance to the securities industry.

The Finance MBA's Job Description

Describe the career path and corresponding responsibilities for an MBA at your firm.

Full-time associates receive global finance training in such areas as investment banking and sales and trading through our associates program. As a sales and trading associate, individuals undergo a six-month training program during which they rotate through various sales and trading areas and participate in intensive product training seminars. In investment banking, associates are expected to become a contributing member of the department immediately. Most of the training is conducted on the job by teaming senior executives in the department with the associates. Since the firm encourages initiative, the degree of responsibility of an associate's assignment is determined to a large extent by an individual's desire and ability to learn and contribute.

The Recruiting Process

Describe your recruiting process and the criteria by which you select candidates. Are grades a criterion? Is prior experience necessary?

NSI seeks people with strong academic records and excellent analytical and communication skills. Demonstration of leadership, high levels of self-motivation, initiative, and commitment, and the ability to work effectively with others in an intense and demanding environment are crucial.

Do you have a summer program for associates or analysts? If so, please describe.

NSI's summer associate program provides a select group of students with an intense, hands-on view of the securities industry, as well as the extensive global operations at Nomura. After choosing to work in one of the following areas—investment banking, derivative products or fixed income, or equity sales and trading—the summer associate is quickly integrated into the department's daily operations. In sales and trading, there is a rotation through the different sales and trading areas. Investment banking and derivative products tend to be more project oriented. Additionally, through a series of weekly seminars with senior managers, the MBAs have the opportunity to be exposed to the many facets of our business.

What international opportunities does your firm offer for U.S. citizens? For foreign nationals?

NSI does not recruit for the other overseas offices. Individuals interested in working internationally should contact NSI for additional information.

Piper Jaffray Inc.

222 South Ninth Street
Minneapolis, MN 55402
(612) 342-6000

MBA Recruiting Contact(s):
Mark Copman, Vice President

Company Description

Describe your firm's business and the types of clients served by your finance group(s).

Piper Jaffray Inc., a full-service investment banking firm headquartered in Minneapolis, is one of the leading investment banks based outside New York City. Established in 1895, it has over 2,400 employees. Piper Jaffray services consist of Equity and Fixed Income Capital Markets, Asset Management with over $10 billion under management, and Retail Distribution, with 875 brokers located in 68 offices across the western United States.

Piper Jaffray's capital markets activities encompass corporate finance, equity research, public finance, debt and equity trading, and equity and fixed income sales. The Corporate Finance Department consists of 35 professionals who are divided along industry or functional specialties. The Research Department has 25 professionals who, with their Corporate Finance peers, lead industry teams. Piper Jaffray has five industry teams—Healthcare, Financial Services, Technology, Consumer, and Food and Agribusiness—as well as functional specialists performing private placements, mergers and acquisitions, venture capital, and valuations. The majority of these services originate from the company's Minneapolis headquarters.

Describe your ownership structure.

Piper Jaffray's stock is listed on the New York Stock Exchange. Approximately 42% of the company's common shares are owned by its employee stock ownership trust. Another 18% is held by employees directly.

How does your approach to finance differ from that of other firms, and what do you consider to be your strengths and distinctive capabilities?

The ownership structure of Piper Jaffray is a distinctive strength. Because much of Piper Jaffray's equity is broadly owned by its employees, there is a strong sense of loyalty to the company and commitment to its professionalism and profitability. Consistent with its focus on servicing the financial needs of emerging-growth companies, Piper Jaffray is also able to commit its own capital to new ventures. It has made a number of venture capital investments in recent years and intends to increase investment in this area in the future.

Piper Jaffray places strong emphasis on the importance of long-term investment banking relationships. The company devotes substantial resources to trading, research coverage, and corporate finance expertise to provide its investment banking clients with the highest levels of service. Piper Jaffray also has one of the industry's lowest turnover rates, which is important to maintaining long-term banking commitments.

The Finance MBA's Job Description

Describe the career path and corresponding responsibilities for an MBA at your firm.

Piper Jaffray emphasizes hiring good people and giving them as much freedom and responsibility as is possible, consistent with general corporate objectives, to determine their own focus and goals. The good people rise to the top on their own initiative, and they remain with Piper Jaffray, in many instances because no other organization can offer them as much latitude to exercise their initiative. This unstructured atmosphere and emphasis on the individual, coupled with our employee ownership structure, have made it possible for entrepreneurial people to satisfy many of their goals within the corporate structure. For example, the Corporate Finance Department has built a partnership mechanism whereby its people, along with other members of management, can build capital by participating in some of the investment opportunities developed in the department.

New Associates are hired as generalists and given substantial latitude to develop industry expertise and functional specialties that are compatible with their particular interests and capabilities. Associates are immediately assigned to a wide variety of projects and given as much responsibility as their experience and capabilities permit. A senior officer in the department supervises all client relationships and engagements. Associates generally choose a particular industry or functional specialty area after a couple of years at Piper Jaffray.

The Recruiting Process

Describe your recruiting process and the criteria by which you select candidates. Are grades a criterion? Is prior experience necessary?

The most successful people in Corporate Finance have come to Piper Jaffray with some significant financially related working experience. This experience has enabled them to contribute effectively to the department at an early stage in their development. Members of the group also must have the confidence, maturity, and personal attributes necessary to develop successful client relationships. In most instances, the current professionals in the department are people who have spent time in financial centers such as New York, or would have done so, but preferred the working environment and growth opportunities that a smaller organization can offer and the lifestyle available in the Twin Cities or Seattle area.

In a typical year, how many permanent associates and analysts do you hire? Do you have a summer program for associates or analysts? If so, please describe.

New Associates are hired primarily into the Corporate Finance Department. Because of the department's size, it is not possible to offer a formal training program. Piper Jaffray typically hires two to five MBA graduates each year.

Piper Jaffray has no organized summer program.

Raymond James & Associates, Inc.

800 Carillon Parkway
St. Petersburg, FL 33716
(813) 573-3800

MBA Recruiting Contact(s):
Gary A. Downing, Managing Director
Corporate Finance
Robert F. Shuck, Vice Chairman
Raymond James Financial

Company Description

Describe your firm's business and the types of clients served by your finance group(s).

Raymond James & Associates is a leading securities firm that offers comprehensive financial services to individuals, corporations, municipalities, and institutions. Since our founding in 1962, Raymond James has grown dramatically by providing these services to our clients and customers with a superior level of execution and integrity. Today, Raymond James is the largest investment banking and brokerage firm headquartered in the Southeast and maintains one of the largest retail brokerage networks in the United States.

Raymond James & Associates provides investment banking services to emerging-growth and established companies throughout the country and in Europe. Both private and public companies are clients. The primary emphasis is on companies within a limited number of industries where sufficient industry knowledge has been developed to deliver an extremely high level of value-added service. Florida and southeastern companies are also well represented on our client list due to geographic location. Investment banking services include public underwritings; private placements; merger, acquisition, and divestiture representation; and various advisory services.

Describe your ownership structure.

Raymond James Financial, the parent company of Raymond James & Associates, is a public corporation and its shares are traded on the New York Stock Exchange.

How does your approach to finance differ from that of other firms, and what do you consider to be your strengths and distinctive capabilities?

Raymond James has developed a reputation for providing capital and advice to emerging-growth and medium-size companies in a limited number of industries. Members of the Investment Banking Department work closely with our highly acclaimed Research Department to develop an in-depth understanding of our clients and their businesses. This allows a high level of value-added services to be provided to the client.

Discuss changes in your firm's revenues (both domestic and international) and professional staff over the past year; over the past five years.

Raymond James is one of the leading growth companies in the country with a compound growth rate in revenues and earnings in excess of 25% per year during the past 15 years. In our most recently completed fiscal year, revenues exceeded $360 million, and profits exceeded $40 million. All major areas of the firm have grown dramatically in the past five years, including expansion of our institutional sales effort to six offices in Europe. The Investment Banking Department has grown from 5 to 15 professionals in the past five years. The number of transactions completed and revenues generated by the Investment Banking Department has also increased dramatically over the past five years.

The Finance MBA's Job Description

Describe the career path and corresponding responsibilities for an MBA at your firm.

Raymond James hires MBAs for a variety of positions within the firm. The most common position is as an Associate within the Investment Banking Department. As an Associate, the recently hired MBA will receive broad exposure to a variety of transactions within a specific industry group. Increased responsibility and client contact occur quickly, assuming the Associate performs well and displays the necessary skills. MBAs can also be hired into Public Finance, Research, Sales and Trading, and Administrative positions.

Describe the opportunities for professional mobility between the various departments in your firm.

There are numerous examples of MBAs' moving from one department to another within the firm as their interests change. Our philosophy is to hire people who are highly qualified and choose to live in Florida for the lifestyle alternative. Thus, we are flexible in meeting their needs over time in recognition of their contributions to the success of the firm.

Discuss the lifestyle aspects of a career with your firm (i.e., average hours per week, amount of travel, flexibility to change offices, corporate culture, etc.).

Raymond James offers an attractive alternative to the lifestyle offered by the major firms in New York. A typical workweek is 60–70 hours, and travel ranges from 40–50%. The real benefit is returning to the warm climate of Florida, where many leisure activities can be pursued year-round. The corporate culture at Raymond James can best be described as, "work hard, play hard."

The Recruiting Process

Describe your recruiting process and the criteria by which you select candidates. Are grades a criterion? Is prior experience necessary?

Raymond James seeks individuals with a track record of superior achievement who wish to work in an entrepreneurial environment in the Southeast. All aspects of a candidate's background are considered and measured against a high set of standards. Personality fit is also an important factor. Prior experience is not required.

RBC Dominion Securities Inc.

P.O. Box 21
Commerce Court South
Toronto, Ontario M5L 1A7
Canada
(416) 864-3932
Fax: (416) 864-4143

MBA Recruiting Contact(s):
R. Jamie Anderson
Vice President and Director

Company Description

Describe your firm's business and the types of clients served by your finance group(s).

RBC Dominion Securities is a fully integrated Canadian investment bank that enjoys a leading position in all segments of the securities business in Canada. With an equity on capital base of more than Cdn. $250 million, the company is the most strongly capitalized Canadian securities firm. Its principal investment banking activities are general corporate and government finance, mergers and acquisitions, corporate restructuring, real estate, fixed income and equity sales and trading, international financing, commercial paper, and foreign exchange. The firm has an extensive retail sales network of 800 registered representatives located in 70 cities across Canada. RBC Dominion Securities also has a strong international presence, with offices in New York, Boston, London, Paris, Lausanne, Hong Kong, Tokyo, and Sydney.

RBC Dominion Securities, founded before the turn of the century, has grown through a series of mergers over the last two decades to become not only the largest investment bank in Canada but also one of the most profitable. The firm's investment banking clients now include most of Canada's largest and fastest-growing companies, as well as ten Canadian provinces, the federal government, and numerous government agencies. In 1990, 1991, and 1992, RBC Dominion Securities lead-managed over 40% of all public Canadian corporate debt and equity offerings in Canada, more than its next two largest competitors combined. The firm has demonstrated a consistent ability to meet the changing needs of its many clients while maintaining a superior rate of return on its own capital. RBC Dominion Securities has been able to take advantage of its strong capital base and exceptional distribution capability to compete effectively and profitably.

The firm's corporate strategy is to be the leading investment bank to Canadian clients in both domestic and international markets and to be the leading investment bank to foreign clients in the Canadian market. The firm achieves this goal through its ability to view client interests as paramount and to deliver superior services that integrate the various areas of strength throughout the firm. This integrated, client-oriented approach has distinguished RBC Dominion Securities in terms of both its reputation and its performance over the past several years.

Describe your ownership structure.

As a consequence of financial services deregulation in Canada, the firm sold a 75% equity interest to the Royal Bank of Canada, Canada's largest commercial bank, in March 1988. The transaction provided the firm with access to the Royal's formidable international network, as well as the financial backing of a major international financial institution with Cdn. $138 billion in assets and Cdn. $6 billion in equity capital. The remaining 25% of RBC Dominion Securities' shares are owned by employees and traded at book value. Associates in investment banking are typically first offered an opportunity to purchase shares in the firm within the first two to three years of their careers.

Unlike some other commercial bank–investment bank ownership relationships in Canada, RBC Dominion Securities has maintained complete independence of operations. No Royal Bank executives have taken positions at RBC Dominion Securities, and the bank fills only 2 of 15 positions on the firm's Board of Directors. Career opportunities and compensation structures for professional staff have and will remain unchanged.

The Finance MBA's Job Description

Describe the career path and corresponding responsibilities for an MBA at your firm.

The firm employs approximately 90 investment banking professionals located in Toronto, Montreal, Calgary, Vancouver, Regina, and New York, as well as in London and other overseas offices. RBC Dominion Securities devotes a great deal of time and consideration to its search for Associates. The firm's intention is to hire outstanding graduates who will continue with the firm throughout their careers. It has among the lowest turnover rates in the industry, primarily because of its determination to ensure that each person is exposed to work with a large number of experienced senior bankers.

Associates who join the investment banking group at RBC Dominion Securities generally do not specialize in any one particular industry or product group. The firm prefers to develop well-rounded professionals who have participated in a wide variety of transactions, whether debt or equity, domestic or international, private or public. Associates are nevertheless encouraged to develop expertise in areas that interest them, and the firm makes every effort to satisfy a professional's ambitions in a particular specialty area. The firm is large enough in Canada to be able to offer both a generalist approach to the business and the opportunity to specialize in specific areas of interest.

Other aspects of RBC Dominion Securities are of interest to potential associates, including the firm's reputation for excellence, innovation, and high ethical standards. Moreover, there are comparatively few Associates, which results in new professionals' being given substantial responsibilities early in their careers. Because RBC Dominion Securities enjoys the lead position in the domestic underwriting league tables, new Associates experience the deal flow necessary to develop well-rounded professionals skills in their early years.

Discuss the lifestyle aspects of a career with your firm (i.e., average hours per week, amount of travel, flexibility to change offices, corporate culture, etc.).

An open and collegial atmosphere prevails throughout the firm. There is a genuine concern on the part of senior management that young professionals develop a number of outside interests and have the ability to devote a significant portion of time to their families. While the highest value is placed on productive output by professionals, the firm does not encourage long hours when they are unnecessary.

The Recruiting Process

Describe your recruiting process and the criteria by which you select candidates. Are grades a criterion? Is prior experience necessary?

RBC Dominion Securities is highly selective in its hiring program. The firm has made a consistent commitment over the years to hire from top business schools in both North America and Europe. A number of criteria are applied, including academic excellence, energetic presentation, evidence of strong outside interests, and overall fit with the firm. Grades by themselves are not given undue consideration. No prior investment banking experience is necessary, and the firm encourages applicants from a wide variety of academic disciplines and work experience. Successful candidates are typically persistent self-starters with a keen interest in financial markets and a good sense of humor.

In a typical year, how many permanent associates and analysts do you hire? Do you have a summer program for associates or analysts? If so, please describe.

Each year two to four full-time Associates and a smaller number of Summer Associates are hired into investment banking. There is no formal training program. Associates are immediately assigned to client transaction teams to learn on the job.

The Robinson-Humphrey Company, Inc.

Atlanta Financial Center
3333 Peachtree Road, NE
Atlanta, GA 30326
(404) 266-6000

MBA Recruiting Contact(s):
Ed McCrady, Vice President
(404) 266-6603

Company Description

Describe your firm's business and the types of clients served by your finance group(s).

The Corporate Finance Department at Robinson-Humphrey consists of 25 professionals. The entire department is located in Robinson-Humphrey's headquarters in Atlanta. Essentially, everyone in the Corporate Finance Department is regarded as a generalist in terms of type of project. Teams of professionals focus on certain industries (e.g., technology, health care, retailing, financial institutions), but a flexible approach to industry coverage is maintained. Robinson-Humphrey attempts to position itself as a complete investment banker to its clients, most of them located in the Southeast. Robinson-Humphrey's primary corporate finance clientele is middle-market, emerging-growth companies based in the Southeast, although the firm does maintain investment banking relationships with several large corporations headquartered in the region. The firm's experience in serving certain industry segments has enabled it to increase its client base outside the Southeast as well.

Describe your ownership structure.

The Robinson-Humphrey Company, Inc. was purchased by American Express in 1982. The firm operates today as a wholly owned subsidiary of Shearson Lehman Brothers, Inc.

How does your approach to finance differ from that of other firms, and what do you consider to be your strengths and distinctive capabilities?

Robinson-Humphrey attempts to position itself as a full-service investment bank to emerging-growth companies, predominantly in the Southeast. Because of its outstanding retail distribution system (47 branches across nine states), as well as its ability to tap the worldwide resources of Shearson Lehman Brothers, Robinson-Humphrey has capabilities unique among regional investment banking firms. The Corporate Finance Department has grown from approximately 15 people to 25 people over the past five years. Robinson-Humphrey is the largest corporate finance and investment banking operation in the Southeast, an area realizing tremendous gains in economic growth and in the origination of capital.

Discuss changes in your firm's revenues (both domestic and international) and professional staff over the past year; over the past five years.

Robinson-Humphrey, like most other investment banking firms, has benefited over the past year from the surge in public underwriting activity. Robinson-Humphrey has been a particularly active underwriter of new equity issues, both initial public offerings and issues for companies whose stocks are already publicly traded. The Corporate Finance Department, however, still maintains a balance between public underwriting and other activities, such as mergers and acquisitions and private capital raising. Over the past five years, merger and acquisition work has comprised from 20% to 80% of the department's business.

This past year the department's professional staff has grown to 25 professionals. Two senior bankers were hired laterally, and two new associates joined the firm during the summer of 1992. These additions continue the growth that the department has experienced during the past five years.

The Finance MBA's Job Description

Describe the career path and corresponding responsibilities for an MBA at your firm.

An Associate works as a key member of transaction teams typically comprising of two to three professionals. The Associate's primary responsibilities consist of transaction execution duties, including financial analysis and project management. The Associate also works with senior professionals to develop new business by meeting with and making presentations to prospective clients. An Associate's degree of responsibility depends on the type and scope of a project and on his or her particular capabilities.

Describe the opportunities for professional mobility between the various departments in your firm.

There is very little mobility between the various departments within Robinson-Humphrey.

Discuss the lifestyle aspects of a career with your firm (i.e., average hours per week, amount of travel, flexibility to change offices, corporate culture, etc.).

People who work at Robinson-Humphrey generally seem to enjoy the lifestyle offered by a career with the firm and fostered by its location in the Southeast. In addition, the relatively small size of the department and of the firm by Wall Street standards tends to encourage close relationships among co-workers. While investment banking inevitably demands a significant time commitment, one's average hours worked and travel schedule will vary depending on market conditions and the number and types of projects on which one is working.

The Recruiting Process

Describe your recruiting process and the criteria by which you select candidates. Are grades a criterion? Is prior experience necessary?

The company hires graduating MBAs to entry-level positions every year, depending on market conditions. Our annual recruiting effort usually begins in the fall, when we solicit cover letters and résumés from interested, qualified candidates. In the past we have not scheduled on-campus recruiting visits, and we do not anticipate a change in that policy. Typically, an entering MBA will have some experience in investment banking or a closely related financial services business. All factors such as grades, prior experience, and personal attributes are taken into consideration in the decision process. However, final recruiting decisions are based on interviews with several people in the department who make judgments concerning a candidate's ability to make a meaningful contribution to the department.

In a typical year, how many permanent associates and analysts do you hire? Do you have a summer program for associates or analysts? If so, please describe.

Hiring decisions are based solely on current and perceived market conditions and an assessment of the department's overall needs. The department has hired from one to three Associates each of the past four years. Most likely, we will hire at least one entry-level MBA in the upcoming year.

The firm does not have a summer program and does not interview for Summer Associates or analysts.

Rothschild Canada Limited

1 First Canadian Place
Suite 3800
P.O. Box 77
Toronto, Ontario M5X 1B1
(416) 369-9600

MBA Recruiting Contact(s):
Gregory A. Milavsky, Vice President

Company Description

Describe your firm's business and the types of clients served by your finance group(s).

Rothschild Canada provides independent investment banking, corporate finance, and financial advisory services to selected Canadian and international clients in Canada and offers the global capability and expertise of the Rothschild Group around the world. Our range of experiences to date includes advising on financings, acquisitions, mergers, divestitures, reorganizations, spin-offs, and, in particular, privatizations and restructurings. In addition, Rothschild Canada is involved in valuing and selling, both nationally and globally, private and public companies as a whole, operating units of large companies, and, in some cases, specific assets.

Rothschild Canada works with the other offices in the Rothschild Group to identify target companies for acquisition or investment purposes for current and prospective clients. There is a steady flow of ideas between Rothschild's offices with respect to opportunities in the mergers and acquisitions market in Canada and internationally.

As part of our long-term relationships with our clients, we advise them on their ongoing corporate and financial strategies and corporate finance activities and on the implementation of their strategic plans.

Rothschild Canada is not associated with commercial banks, financial institutions, or industrial groups in Canada, nor does it engage in public underwriting, market trading, arbitrage, or principal investing. Rothschild Canada is able to provide unbiased judgments free from potential conflicts of interest.

Describe your ownership structure.

Rothschild Canada Limited is the Canadian member of one of the world's leading independent merchant banking organizations, the Rothschild Group. The main op-

erating company of the Rothschild Group in the United Kingdom is N M Rothschild & Sons Limited, the merchant bank that has been based at New Court in the City of London for nearly 200 years. The Rothschild Group has expanded globally to meet the ever more diverse needs of its clients and now has offices in 20 countries worldwide. The Canadian office was opened in 1990 and has grown each year.

How does your approach to finance differ from that of other firms, and what do you consider to be your strengths and distinctive capabilities?

Rothschild Canada's independence and professional client-related approach to its focused business of providing advisory services differentiates it from its competitors in Canada.

The Finance MBA's Job Description

Describe the career path and corresponding responsibilities for an MBA at your firm.

A new member of the investment banking team has the opportunity to gain experience quickly in a vast number of transactions. Our experience to date has covered all major industries in Canada and a wide range of various types of transactions. Our professionals do not specialize in industrial sectors or products, although the majority of our professionals have brought years of experience to Rothschild Canada in all aspects of industry. In particular, the office has developed an expertise in privatizations and debt restructurings of public and private corporations. All professionals begin as generalists, gathering as wide a portfolio of experiences as possible. As the firm grows, professionals naturally develop areas of particular expertise upon which the Canadian office, as well as our international group, will draw in dealing with various clients' needs.

Describe the opportunities for professional mobility between the various departments in your firm.

There are opportunities to meet and work with professionals from Rothschild's other offices, or the Rothschild Group, as well as opportunities to consider extended assignments in other offices.

Discuss the lifestyle aspects of a career with your firm (i.e., average hours per week, amount of travel, flexibility to change offices, corporate culture, etc.).

While the lifestyle of an investment banker is renowned for its hard work and long hours, Rothschild Canada maintains a friendly and cooperative atmosphere. Within a very short period, every new Associate will have worked with all members of the office. The professionals are relatively young, and this allows for common interests and non-work-related activities.

The Recruiting Process

Describe your recruiting process and the criteria by which you select candidates. Are grades a criterion? Is prior experience necessary?

The recruiting process at Rothschild Canada has identified certain characteristics that we feel are crucial to having a successful and long-term career in investment banking. While strong academic performance is not in itself a requirement, it does tend to indicate the dedication and commitment that recruits have made in their past endeavors. Experience in the industry or in related fields will also act as guidance in identifying those recruits who have decided to make investment banking their career choice. A third requirement, of course, is that recruits be able to work in Canada.

S.G. Warburg & Co. Inc.

787 Seventh Avenue
New York, NY 10019
(212) 459-7728
Telex: 170984
Fax: (212) 459-7251

MBA Recruiting Contact(s):
Stephanie C. Flack, Vice President
Director of Human Resources
(212) 459-7183

Company Description

Describe your firm's business and the types of clients served by your finance group(s).

S.G. Warburg & Co. Inc. (the firm) is the U.S. arm of the S.G. Warburg Group plc (the Group), a preeminent international investment banking and securities organization with over 5200 employees in 20 countries. The Group is a world leader in mergers and acquisitions, international equities, and a wide range of international fixed income products. Its subsidiary, Mercury Asset Management Group plc, is one of the largest fund managers in the world.

The firm employs over 375 people in our New York headquarters and in Boston, serving corporations ranging from *Fortune* 100 to emerging-growth companies in many industries, as well as pension funds, money managers, and other institutional investors.

Describe your ownership structure.

The S.G. Warburg Group plc is listed on the London Stock Exchange with over 6300 shareholders and approximately 208 million ordinary shares outstanding.

How does your approach to finance differ from that of other firms, and what do you consider to be your strengths and distinctive capabilities?

We combine in-depth knowledge and experience in the United States with unsurpassed global capabilities and acknowledged leadership and innovation in our industry. We are known for our traditions of client commitment and excellence in service.

Underpinning the Group's global organization is an unparalleled network of investment banking, merger and acquisition, and equity research services located in key markets, including the U.K., Germany, France, Spain, Italy, Canada, and Australia. This network is fully integrated and organized along functional lines to ensure that resources are marshaled effectively to help clients meet their objectives.

The Group has been recognized for its preeminence in cross-border mergers and acquisitions and was ranked number one in European cross-border transactions completed in 1991. In addition, we were ranked number one in companies covered on an equity research basis worldwide as well as number one in *Institutional Investor*'s All-Europe Research Team, a survey of nearly 500 institutions in 22 countries. The Group's fixed income research is consistently highly rated by the most respected independent surveys of institutional investors.

Discuss changes in your firm's revenues (both domestic and international) and professional staff over the past year; over the past five years.

Over the last 12 months, S.G. Warburg & Co. Inc. has increased its level of activity in the United States dramatically. Over 43 U.S. investment banking professionals have generated a record number of managed and comanaged deals valued at approximately U.S. $2 billion.

The Finance MBA's Job Description

Describe the career path and corresponding responsibilities for an MBA at your firm.

The divisions into which MBAs are hired are Advisory and Financing (investment banking) and Equities.

The Group's investment banking division is represented in all major financial centers throughout the world, and its members are organized in general corporate advisory teams and more specialized financing teams. Most MBA graduates join financing teams that are responsible for the marketing and execution of the full range of financing services, including equity and debt insurance, lending, leasing, and project finance. The general corporate advisory teams are organized along client and geographical lines. Members provide financial advice to their clients on a wide range of topics, including mergers, acquisitions, and financial restructuring, and are the primary point of contact for the provision of the division's advisory and financing services.

The Equities division distributes, trades, and researches equities in the U.S. and international markets. Graduates are hired for positions in research analysis, sales, or trading. Sales professionals provide institutional investors with the advice and service needed to make and implement their investment decisions. Research analysts provide perspective on global sectors, markets, and industries irrespective of national boundaries. This analysis supports the sales force in making their investment recommendations to investors. The sales force also provides feedback to issuers on market sentiment.

Describe the opportunities for professional mobility between the various departments in your firm.

Interdepartmental movement throughout careers is encouraged to widen experience and knowledge. The diversity of the Group requires that we be active in managing the career development and training of our professionals and in increasing their mobility between divisions and geographic locations. This is important to the success of the Group as a whole as well as to the individual.

Discuss the lifestyle aspects of a career with your firm (i.e., average hours per week, amount of travel, flexibility to change offices, corporate culture, etc.).

The work environment at S.G. Warburg is best characterized as one in which high intellectual standards, a meritocracy, rigorous attention to detail, and a strong emphasis on teamwork are combined. Due to the highly international nature of our work, travel is very much an integral part of the new graduate's job activities.

The Recruiting Process

Describe your recruiting process and the criteria by which you select candidates.

S.G. Warburg seeks to hire creative individuals with high overall achievement levels who are willing and able to work together as a team.

In a typical year, how many permanent associates and analysts do you hire? Do you have a summer program for associates or analysts? If so, please describe.

S.G. Warburg has a full-time associate and analyst recruiting program. The Group hires new associates according to need and does not maintain a quota of new hires per year.

What international opportunities does your firm offer for U.S. citizens? For foreign nationals?

Opportunities exist for internal transfers to our locations overseas for both U.S. citizens and foreign nationals dependent upon business needs, work experience, and performance while in the New York office. Those interested primarily in opportunities abroad should contact New York for further information.

Salomon Brothers Inc

Seven World Trade Center
New York, NY 10048
(212) 783-7000

MBA Recruiting Contact(s):
Christine A. Simpson, Vice President
Investment Banking Recruiting
(212) 783-5923
Fax: (212) 783-3350

Penley Toffolon, Vice President
Sales and Trading Recruiting
(212) 783-6186
Fax: (212) 783-2342

Company Description

Describe your firm's business and the types of clients served by your finance group(s).

Salomon Brothers is a full-service financial institution engaged in investment banking, market making and trading of financial instruments, fixed income and equity market research, and institutional money management. Salomon's services and activities include advisory services provided for mergers and acquisitions and financial restructurings; capital-raising activities, including the underwriting and distribution of debt, equity, and derivative securities; trading and arbitrage strategies using debt, equity, and derivative instruments; entering into contractual commitments, such as forward securities and currency agreements, interest rate swap, cap, and floor agreements; options, warrants, and derivative products; fixed income and equity market research; institutional money management services; precious metals trading; and mortgage banking. Salomon Brothers conducts its business globally, with offices in Australia, Canada, France, Germany, Hong Kong, Japan, Singapore, South Korea, Spain, Switzerland, Taiwan, Thailand, the United Kingdom, and the United States. Its customer base consists primarily of large- and medium-size corporations, governments, and financial institutions. Financial services are also provided to individuals on a limited basis.

Investment Banking

Salomon Brothers' investment banking activities consist principally of raising capital and providing strategic advisory services. Capital-raising activities include underwriting and distributing debt and equity securities and involve the development, underwriting, and distribution of derivative products. These products include warrants linked to a variety of instruments, such as debt securities, equity securities, baskets of equity securities, indexes based upon stock markets throughout the world, and commodities such as gold and oil. Strategic advisory services are provided in connection with mergers and acquisitions, leveraged buyouts, financial restructurings, and privatizations.

Sales and Trading

Salomon Brothers is a major dealer in government securities in New York, Tokyo, London, and Frankfurt and is a member of major international securities, financial futures, and options exchanges. It has extensive distribution capabilities and one of the largest capital bases in the U.S. securities industry. Salomon Brothers is a major underwriter of securities for governments and high-grade primary issuers and is capable of executing trading strategies on behalf of its customers and for its own account requiring significant commitments of capital.

Salomon's trading expertise, which dates back more than 80 years, together with the ability to execute a high volume of transactions with counterparties, enables it to provide liquidity to investors across a broad range of markets and financial instruments. Salomon Brothers' ability to execute arbitrage strategies is enhanced not only by its established presence in international capital markets but also by its utilization of information technology, quantitative methods, and risk management tools; its research capabilities; and its leadership position in the development and use of financial derivative products.

Describe your ownership structure.

Salomon Brothers Inc is the investment banking/brokerage subsidiary of Salomon Inc, a New York Stock Exchange–listed firm. A substantial portion of Salomon Inc's equity is owned by its employees and Berkshire Hathaway, Inc. In 1990, Salomon Inc implemented the Equity Partnership Plan for Key Employees (EPP), designed to provide participants, including newly hired MBAs, with a continuing long-term investment in common stock of Salomon Inc. Through the EPP and other programs designed to increase employee ownership, Salomon Inc expects that within the next few years, its employees will own 30% of the firm's common stock.

How does your approach to finance differ from that of other firms, and what do you consider to be your strengths and distinctive capabilities?

Several areas of competence distinguish the businesses of Salomon Inc: our ability and willingness to commit capital for our clients and for ourselves; our superior risk management and financial engineering capabilities; our geographic breadth, with strong customer and proprietary businesses on four continents; our first-class financial advisory and analytical skills and databases; and the character of our professionals.

Discuss changes in your firm's revenues (both domestic and international) and professional staff over the past year; over the past five years.

The financial services industry is characterized by change. Increasingly, the businesses of Salomon Brothers are becoming global. A number of products, markets, and clients that contribute significantly to the revenue and profitability of Salomon Brothers today were nonexistent five years ago. The establishment of a Tokyo office, where Salomon Brothers has become the leading non-Japanese competitor in terms of both revenue and profitability, and the development of its derivative product businesses are illustrative of such markets and products. A hallmark of Salomon Brothers has been its willingness to commit capital, both financial and human, to the development of promising emerging businesses such as these.

As of April 30, 1993, Salomon Brothers employed approximately 6,500 employees worldwide, approximately the same number employed as of December 31, 1986.

The Finance MBA's Job Description

Describe the career path and corresponding responsibilities for an MBA at your firm. Describe the opportunities for professional mobility between the various departments in your firm.

New Associates, as well as senior investment bankers, have identified career mobility, cohesiveness, early professional responsibility, and comprehensive training as salient considerations in their decision to join Salomon Brothers.

Flexibility and Options
Flexibility is the hallmark of a professional career at Salomon Brothers. In Investment Banking, several options are available. During the recruiting process, new Associates may choose corporate finance or financial institutions. In contrast with a number of other major investment banks, Salomon does not compel a candidate to choose a specific functional specialty in order to get an offer.

Most of the Associates who join Investment Banking enter the generalist associate program, where they have the opportunity to work with many product and coverage areas to develop a broad banking competence. During their first year at the firm, generalists typically spend approximately 25% of their time on financings, 30% on mergers and acquisitions assignments, 25% on financial advisory and restructuring work, and 20% on business development.

After their first one to two years in Corporate Finance, Associates usually select an initial specialization that best fits their interest and background. Areas of specialization include the following:

> Capital Market Services (synthesizes the efforts of Corporate Finance, Sales, and Trading in new product development and public debt offerings)
> Mergers and Acquisitions
> Leveraged Finance
> Specialty Industries (i.e., media, telecommunications and technology, forest products/paper, retailing, transportation, utilities, and regional industrial and high-yield coverage in the eastern United States)
> Specialty Finance Products (high yield, private placements, project finance, and leasing)
> International (coverage of foreign and international corporations and governments: London, Tokyo, Frankfurt, Sydney, New York)

After three years in Financial Institutions, Associates also select an initial specialization. Areas of initial specialization include the following:

> Commercial Bank Coverage, Insurance Coverage, or Finance Company Coverage
> Lease Finance
> Structured Project Finance
> Receivables and Diversified
> Structured Mortgage Finance
> Government Finance
> Real Estate Finance

Similarly, Salomon takes the generalist approach in hiring for sales and trading. All interns are recruited for the training program and then choose their areas of specialty after exposure to all facets of sales and trading through our intensive training and rotation process. These areas of specialization include the following:

> Equity Sales
> Equity Trading
> Fixed-Income Sales
> Government Bonds
> Corporate Bonds
> Mortgage Bonds

Interest-Rate Swaps
Futures and Options
Foreign Exchange
Fixed-Income Trading
Asset/Liability Management

A career at Salomon Brothers is dynamic. Many of today's most important product lines and services either did not exist or were relatively small portions of our business a few years ago. Many of our people are now working in product areas that did not exist at the time they joined the firm. We are confident that Salomon's flexibility will enable the organization to continue to capitalize on emerging market opportunities and challenges.

Integration and Teamwork

The integration of the firm's investment banking, research, sales, and trading capabilities is responsible for Salomon's performance. Our achievements reflect the combined expertise of many areas within Finance, as well as contributions from other departments and our international network.

Teamwork is ingrained in Salomon Brothers' professionals. Investment Banking professionals work closely with members of the Sales, Trading, and Syndicate departments on the trading floor, as well as with Research. For example, while working on an initial public offering, an Associate will interact extensively with Syndicate, Equity Sales, and Stock Research.

Salomon's performance-based compensation policy underscores the fact that teamwork and cooperation are the basis of our business success. Unlike many of its competitors, Salomon Brothers does not pay commissions to sales and trading professionals. Instead, a broad group of senior managers carefully assesses each person's contributions to the firm's overall performance.

Responsibility and Participation

Although the number of professionals has grown to meet new market opportunities, Salomon remains committed to a leanly staffed organization. The firm emphasizes small working groups that give new Associates room in which to operate and develop.

A first-year finance Associate works closely with a Managing Director and a Vice President on each of his or her important assignments. Rapid client responsibility is encouraged. We are anxious to bring new Associates into client contact at the earliest possible stage so that they will cultivate the relationships that are critical to the firm's long-term success.

In Sales and Trading, a first-year Associate's exposure to Managing Directors and Vice Presidents is also immediate. Sales units and trading desks are run by Managing Directors who spend most of their time on the sales or trading desk. Furthermore, sales units and trading desks are broken down into small subunits run by experienced Vice Presidents who act as mentors to train the young Associates. Salespeople are given account assignments soon after their placement on a desk, and traders receive risk-taking responsibilities at a very rapid pace. Hands-on training and significant early responsibility are hallmarks of the Salomon sales and trading program.

The Recruiting Process

Describe your recruiting process and the criteria by which you select candidates. Are grades a criterion? is prior experience necessary?

Salomon's character is reflected in the diversity, talents, and various backgrounds of its new Associates. Salomon recruits Associates who have displayed exceptional talent at whatever they have set their minds to. Rather than seeking a particular résumé, experience, or personality, we look for individuals with a proved record of achievement, entrepreneurial initiative, outstanding integrity, and continuing desire to work hard and excel. Salomon's 1993 class includes representatives from a large number of business, law, and other graduate schools, of which a significant proportion were international.

In a typical year, how many permanent associates and analysts do you hire? Do you have a summer program for associates or analysts? If so, please describe.

Professional development has always been a top priority of the firm. New members of all departments—from Investment Banking and Research to Sales and Trading—complete the firm's training program, widely considered the broadest in scope and most challenging of its kind on Wall Street. The program has three basic components:

1. Two months of classroom training, which is conducted at the firm's New York headquarters for all new Associates in Investment Banking and Sales and Trading worldwide. Senior managers provide instruction on all firm capabilities and organizations. Trainees are expected to complete assignments and rotate responsibilities for monitoring and summarizing market activities to the class each morning.

2. Rotation among sales and trading desks in key product areas to work alongside senior managers.

3. Preparation for the Registered Representative examination given by the National Association of Securities Dealers and the New York Stock Exchange.

Training modules continue for three weeks in Investment Banking and eight weeks in Sales and Trading.

Salomon Brothers' compensation policy reflects the firm's belief in a team approach to business. Bonuses and salaries are based on each professional's overall contribution to the firm's performance, which includes such factors as creativity and imagination, management potential, and the ability to train others within the firm.

In a typical year, how many permanent associates and analysts do you hire? Do you have a summer program for associates or analysts? If so, please describe.

In 1994 our Investment Banking Department plans to hire approximately 18–20 summer and 20–25 full-time Associates. In addition, our Sales and Trading Department estimates that it will hire 10–15 summer and 10–15 full-time MBA candidates.

The Salomon summer program is designed to identify candidates for full-time positions. More than 75% of Salomon Summer Associates have received offers, filling approximately half of our full-time hiring needs.

The Investment Banking summer program provides a realistic introduction to the firm and work experience comparable to that of a full-time Associate. Summer professionals function as full-time Associates and become integral team members working on financings, mergers and acquisitions, and new business presentations.

The Sales and Trading summer program is a flexible, unstructured program that allows Associates to rotate to different areas of the firm in both equities and fixed income. Presentations and product-specific classes are an integral part of the program, giving the Associate an introduction to a full range of security products, as well as a realistic experience in Sales and Trading.

What international opportunities does your firm offer for U.S. citizens? For foreign nationals?

Salomon Brothers' Investment Banking operations in Asia include offices in Bangkok, Melbourne, Seoul, Singapore, Sydney, Taipei, and Tokyo and affiliations in Bombay and Kuala Lumpur. In addition, there are professionals based in our New York office who are dedicated to servicing the requirements of our Asian clients in the United States. This network enables Salomon to maintain regular contact with governments and major industrial and financial institutions throughout the region. These offices are staffed with Investment Banking professionals with both regional and product expertise, including capital markets, mergers and acquisitions, project and lease finance, and real estate.

Europe is a key component of Salomon Brothers' global investment banking network. Salomon Brothers' activities in Europe are headquartered in London, and Salomon Brothers is also supported by offices in Berlin, Frankfurt, Madrid, Milan, Paris, and Zurich. In Europe Salomon Brothers provides a full range of investment banking services to corporations and to sovereign and supranational organizations. The Investment Banking group in London is staffed primarily by European nationals and includes individuals from over a dozen countries. Salomon Brothers' continuing commitment to Europe reflects the importance of the European economies on the world stage and the vital role Europe plays in the international financial markets.

For further information contact Tracy Parnell, Salomon Brothers International Limited, Victoria Plaza, 111 Buckingham Palace Road, London SW1W 0SB England.

Simmons & Company International

700 Louisiana
Suite 4900
Houston, TX 77002
(713) 236-9999

MBA Recruiting Contact(s):
Matthew R. Simmons, President (HBS MBA '67)
J. Kevin Bartol, Vice President (HBS MBA '85)
Nancy A. Keegan, Vice President (HBS MBA '88)

Company Description

Describe your firm's business and the types of clients served by your finance group(s). Describe your ownership structure.

Simmons & Company International is a privately owned investment banking firm based in Houston. Since the firm's founding in 1974, Simmons has provided corporate finance advisory services exclusively to the international oil and gas service and equipment industry. Simmons is one of a limited number of investment banking firms not based in New York City whose business primarily consists of executing complex corporate finance transactions and undertaking complicated financial engineering assignments for the firm's clients.

The firm limits its activity to mergers and acquisitions advisory services, private placements of debt and equity, financial restructuring advisory work, and a variety of consulting assignments. Simmons has implemented more than 300 transactions having an aggregate value of over $9 billion. Having concentrated exclusively in corporate finance activities for 19 years, the firm is now embarking on an expansion in the institutional sales and research of oil and gas service and equipment company equities.

The firm recently expanded its services to advising institutional clients on direct equity investments in the oil service industry. In partnership with Houston-based Fayez Sarofim & Company, Simmons now advises a $50-million equity fund for oil service investments.

Simmons & Company conducts its business worldwide. Approximately 25% of Simmons's clients are Texas based, 50% are in other parts of the United States, and 25% are international.

Since its founding, Simmons has maintained four overriding corporate goals that define the firm's culture:

1. Specialization. We provide financial services exclusively to the oil and gas service and equipment industry.

2. Quality. We aim to deliver the absolutely highest-quality "product" to our clients.

3. Size. We want to remain a relatively small, highly specialized group of professionals.

4. Culture. We offer a stimulating work environment for our professional staff and those who work with us.

How does your approach to finance differ from that of other firms, and what do you consider to be your strengths and distinctive capabilities?

The key difference and competitive advantage of Simmons & Company is our exclusive focus on the international oil and gas service and equipment industry.

This industry is incredibly diverse, large, and vital to the international economy. It includes any firm that supplies any product or service involved in the exploration, production, transportation, or processing of hydrocarbons. The industry comprises thousands of companies with aggregate estimated annual revenues of $150 billion.

Simmons & Company is considered the preeminent financial advisor to the oil and gas service and equipment industry. Simmons' specialization and unique knowledge base provide a distinctive competitive advantage over the firm's major competitors, the large Wall Street investment banking firms. Our market share for transactions in the oil service industry that are handled by investment banking firms is more than three times any other investment banking firm in the world.

Several other aspects of our business are different from many of our competitors. First, we operate strictly on a team basis, and in any given year, all Associates have the opportunity to participate as a team member with virtually all other professionals in the firm. Second, we maintain strict control over the number and types of projects we undertake and believe that our close rate on committed projects is as high as any other firm in our business. Finally, the depth of our analysis exceeds most of our competition.

Discuss changes in your firm's revenues (both domestic and international) and professional staff over the past year; over the past five years.

The oil and gas service and equipment industry has proved to be one of the most volatile parts of the world economy. The past decade has included a boom and then a depression of a magnitude unprecedented in any other industry in any historical period. This unparalleled volatility has created tremendous opportunities for Simmons & Company. Over the past five years, the firm has approximately doubled its professional staff and revenue base, and growth is expected to continue. However, the firm intends to remain relatively small and specialized. Simmons now includes 4 Partners, 5 Vice Presidents, and a group of 12 Associates and Analysts, plus a support staff of approximately 15.

In late 1992 Simmons established the Institutional Securities division. The focus of this new division is to capitalize on the firm's unique expertise in the oil service industry by providing research on the approximately 90 publicly traded oil service companies and on industry trends to the institutional investor community. Simmons has expanded its services to include participation in public offerings of oil service equities as both an underwriter and comanager. We established a trading and clearing relationship with Morgan Stanley & Company Inc. and plan to expand into market making in over-the-counter stocks in the near term. The Institutional Securities division remains completely focused on the oil service and equipment industry.

The Finance MBA's Job Description

Describe the career path and corresponding responsibilities for an MBA at your firm.

The primary objective for an incoming Associate is to gain the experience, judgment, and maturity to assume a leadership role in managing our projects and to market the firm's services effectively. As an Associate, an MBA can expect to progress through assignments of increasing responsibility toward partnership and ultimate ownership in the firm.

An MBA can expect to have immediate and substantial client contact, including written and oral presentations. Simmons & Company emphasizes analysis, so an Associate should anticipate considerable quantitative work. All projects are organized on a team basis, with one or more Associates and Analysts supporting a Managing Director who serves as project manager. In a typical year, an Associate would work on seven to ten different projects with the other members of a team.

Discuss the lifestyle aspects of a career with your firm (i.e., average hours per week, amount of travel, flexibility to change offices, corporate culture, etc.).

One of Simmons & Company's enduring corporate goals is to offer a stimulating work environment for our professional staff and those who work with us. The work environment is fast-paced and engrossing, and domestic and international travel is involved; however, work hours and travel requirements do not preclude members of the firm from developing outside interests. Perhaps the strongest statement the firm can make about its commitment to provide a stimulating lifestyle is our unusually low turnover among investment banking professionals.

The Recruiting Process

Describe your recruiting process and the criteria by which you select candidates. Are grades a criterion? Is prior experience necessary?

Simmons & Company seeks MBAs with two or more years of professional business experience, strong analytical ability, intellectual curiosity, a desire to work with people, a desire to keep on a fast learning curve, a sense of humor, and, most important, a commitment to excellence. The most important criterion for success is the "chemistry" fit with other members of the firm.

Our professionals come from remarkably diverse backgrounds. No prior exposure to the oil service industry is either required or necessary.

In a typical year, how many permanent associates and analysts do you hire? Do you have a summer program for associates or analysts? If so, please describe.

Because Simmons is, and plans to remain, a relatively small firm, recruiting for Associates is limited. Simmons & Company has no formal summer program for MBAs.

Smith Barney, Harris Upham & Co. Incorporated

1345 Avenue of the Americas
New York, NY 10105
(212) 698-3601

MBA Recruiting Contact(s):
Basil A. Bliss, Vice President

Company Description

Describe your firm's business and the types of clients served by your finance group(s).

Smith Barney, a Primerica subsidiary, has nearly 7,500 employees in 100 offices in the United States and abroad. Its principal businesses are corporate and municipal securities financing, securities brokerage, trading, and the marketing of a wide variety of financial products and services. It serves, as it has for 118 years, corporations and governments, financial institutions, and individuals.

Specialty Groups
The Corporate Finance Department is organized by geographic region, industry specialty and financing, or functional specialty. About two-thirds of the department's professionals are regional generalists or industry specialists who have basic responsibility for developing and maintaining client relationships within their geographic regions or industry areas. These professionals also structure, negotiate, and process a variety of transactions for their clients. When a specialized financing skill is required to meet a client's needs, they will interface between the client and the transaction specialist within the department. The regional and industry specialists are supported by the functional specialty groups that include mergers and acquisitions, private placements, tax-exempt finance, and financial restructuring.

Describe your ownership structure.

For 114 years Smith Barney was a private corporation wholly owned by the firm's active officers. In June 1987, Smith Barney was acquired by Primerica Corporation, a diversified financial services corporation that is the successor to American Can Company. For Smith Barney clients, this acquisition meant access to additional products and services as Smith Barney continued to operate autonomously as Primerica's largest subsidiary. In December 1988, Commercial Credit merged with Primerica.

This new corporation conducts business under the Primerica name and enhances Smith Barney's position as a leader within the financial services industry. The new Primerica, with a market capitalization of over $4.5 billion, is a leading financial services company with activities in investment banking, capital management, insurance, and mortgage banking. The combination has enhanced opportunities for significant professional and business growth for Smith Barney.

How does your approach to finance differ from that of other firms, and what do you consider to be your strengths and distinctive capabilities?

Diversified and Integrated Approach
Smith Barney offers the broad range of investment banking services to its corporate clients and integrates the resources of the firm in its investment banking effort.

This diversification has not only maximized the department's revenue stream but has also reduced the firm's exposure to variations in any single revenue source. This diversification is particularly important to the investment banking effort, since management has achieved an integrated approach where every department within the firm is involved in servicing existing clients and identifying new opportunities.

Broad Capabilities
Smith Barney excels in its traditional underwriting business and is among the leading investment banking firms in mergers, acquisitions, private placements, tax-exempt finance, project and lease finance, real estate finance, and tax-advantaged finance. The firm's ability to serve the financing needs of its clients stems from its highly developed capabilities in the disciplines most important to the success of any public offering:

- Balanced distribution strength. Our retail sales force focuses on high-net-worth retail clients and as such has access to one of the largest pools of retail capital of any other firm on Wall Street. Our institutional sales force consistently ranks in the top tier of every *Institutional Investor*, *Financial World*, and *Greenwich Research Associates* survey.

- Broad trading capability. The firm is a premier market maker in its clients' stock and a major factor in the block trading and execution of listed securities.

- Distinctive research. Smith Barney consistently ranks in the top tier of every *Institutional Investor* survey of Wall Street research departments.

On the international corporate finance front, our professionals provide the full range of advisory and merger and acquisition services. They raise capital in the Yankee

Bond, Asian dollar, and Eurodollar markets and from Middle East funds sources. The firm offers both investment banking and brokerage services through its offices in London, New York, Mexico City, Bahrain, and Tokyo.

Innovative Financing Products

The firm has created and marketed several unique financing products, including cash option warrants, remarketed preferred stock, price protection rights, and share-adjusted broker-remarketed equity securities (SABRES).

Strong Growing Client Base

Smith Barney has a strong and varied client base, ranging from some of the largest companies in the United States and abroad to emerging-growth companies. Many of the firm's clients are leaders in their respective industries, such as Dow Chemical, KLM Royal Dutch Airlines, Bell-South, Southwestern Bell, Mead, Exxon, and Scott Paper Company. Other clients such as Centel Corporation and HEALTHSOUTH Rehabilitation Corporation, are among the fastest-growing companies in the country. Smith Barney is committed to growth companies and understanding their needs.

Unique Corporate Culture

Smith Barney is dedicated to total service and uncompromising professionalism. We have tried to create an environment where dedicated professionals can fulfill their professional goals, earn premium compensation, and enjoy the interpersonal associations that result. The Corporate Finance Department operates as a meritocracy with sufficient opportunity for each professional to advance as far and as fast as his or her individual ambition and capabilities will allow. Our competitive instincts are focused externally rather than internally. We have chosen to work hard and to enjoy our work, our environment, and our co-workers.

Discuss changes in your firm's revenues (both domestic and international) and professional staff over the past year; over the past five years.

Smith Barney's corporate finance staff consists of approximately 215 professionals located in New York, San Francisco, Los Angeles, Dallas, London, and Tokyo. Over 150 professionals are headquartered in New York, about 30 work out of our domestic regional offices, and another 35 are assigned to overseas branches.

The revenues of the Corporate Finance Department have grown steadily and yet dramatically over the last five years. Such growth is attributable to a strategically focused approach to our existing business and an intelligent approach to professional growth and new business. Therefore, unlike a number of our competitors, following

the 1987 October Crash, we did not have to contend with the unpleasant consequences of yesteryear's frenzied and unsustainable growth in professional staff. Our strategy was to grow our staff and our revenue in a deliberate manner. This philosophy has stood us in good stead in the past and will be adhered to in the future.

The Finance MBA's Job Description

Describe the career path and corresponding responsibilities for an MBA at your firm.

The Corporate Finance Department's management is concerned with the successful and rapid development of its corporate finance professionals. Incoming Associates are assigned to client teams and immediately begin working with senior corporate finance professionals on client transactions and new business development. Associates are exposed to all areas of the business and work with as many officers as possible on a variety of transactions.

Describe the opportunities for professional mobility between the various departments in your firm.

After an Associate has developed a solid knowledge of general corporate finance and has demonstrated technical competence and a high degree of professionalism, he or she may wish to capitalize on specific industry or transaction experience and join one of the specialist groups or spend time in one of our domestic or international regional offices.

Discuss the lifestyle aspects of a career with your firm (i.e., average hours per week, amount of travel, flexibility to change offices, corporate culture, etc.).

Success in this industry comes at a price. The work is often rigorous and demanding. It requires intellect, character, and a commitment of time that only a few can muster over the long haul.

If you are among those who are willing and prepared to take on the challenge, Smith Barney offers unique opportunities. We have built our 118-year track record on old-fashioned principles of hard work and providing superior service to our institutional and private clients.

While sticking to our basic values, we have more than kept pace with the revolutionary changes that have swept our business. Today we are a major factor in all aspects of the investment banking and brokerage business. Yet our size means that there is no getting lost in the crowd here. You become part of the Smith Barney team and begin making your contribution on day one.

One of the intangibles that sets Smith Barney apart is the spirit of teamwork and cooperation that pervades the firm. Teamwork is not a nicety. It is a necessity. It means working harder and working smarter, bringing all of the firm's resources to bear on behalf of the client.

The Recruiting Process

Describe your recruiting process and the criteria by which you select candidates. Are grades a criterion? Is prior experience necessary?

In recent years, over 60% of the Corporate Finance Department's new Associates have had experience, either as Summer Associates or as two-year Analysts. The percentage of Summer Associates who have had prior investment banking experience is quite low. The following personality traits are important for Associates:

- Intelligence. The ability to understand a myriad of complex financial, business, and interpersonal situations and to identify actions that will serve the firm and its clients.

- Self-motivation. The ability to identify opportunities to contribute and the initiative to seize such opportunities with a minimum of supervision and structure.

- Dedication. The desire to invest significant time and effort to reach objectives that are important to the individual, the firm, and our clients.

- Efficiency. The ability to organize and direct resources toward accomplishing a number of tasks simultaneously according to appropriate priorities.

- Interpersonal skills. The ability to relate well to people within the firm and within our client companies.

Do you have a summer program for associates or analysts? If so, please describe.

In the past several years, the Corporate Finance Department has sponsored a summer intern program, and we generally hire between six and eight Associates each summer. Summer Associates have worked in New York, Los Angeles, and San Francisco.

The program emphasizes the direct involvement and exposure of the Summer Associates to a variety of activities, including public underwriting, private placements, project finance, mergers and acquisitions, and financial consulting. Summer Associates assume the same responsibilities as full-time Associates: participating in client service teams, planning and conducting presentations, participating in new business activities, and interacting with senior members of the firm. Although the majority of the summer is spent in the Corporate Finance Department, the program includes an opportunity to learn about the activities of the firm's other areas, such as syndicate, trading, and sales.

Because we hope that a successful Summer Associate will return to become a full-time Associate, the qualifications for Summer Associates are the same as those for full-time employment. A strong interest in finance, good interpersonal skills, and an ability to manage time and resources effectively are all important attributes for Summer Associates. Prior financial experience is not a prerequisite to summer employment, although a good foundation in accounting and finance will help Summer Associates learn the analytical tools that are important to corporate finance activities.

Teachers Insurance and Annuity Association-College Retirement Equities Fund (TIAA-CREF)

730 Third Avenue
New York, NY 10017

MBA Recruiting Contact(s):
Robert A. Moll, Human Resources Officer

Company Description

Describe your firm's business and the types of clients served by your finance group(s).

As the world's largest pension fund, with over $116 billion in assets under management, TIAA-CREF professionals skillfully invest in virtually every economic sector. TIAA assets are broadly diversified among private placements, publicly traded bonds, commercial mortgages and real estate. CREF, the companion corporation, is a registered investment company.

Quality and yield are the bedrock of our investment activities. In fact, TIAA is a top performer in the insurance industry, and its strong balance sheets earn the highest possible ratings from Moody's, Standard & Poor's, Duff & Phelps, and A.M. Best.

TIAA-CREF originated a pension system of portable benefits in 1918 to help ensure the financial security of people employed in education and research. Today, over 1.6 million professors, research scientists, and other educators turn to TIAA-CREF for expert benefit counseling, affordable insurance protection, and retirement income that cannot be outlived.

Stable cash flows, innovative strategies, and years of experience make TIAA a leader in direct placement loans to private and public companies, as well as in publicly traded bonds. TIAA also invests in highly structured deals, including private securitized financings, hybrid credit/real estate deals, project financings, and secondary private placements.

The Finance MBA's Job Description

Describe the career path and corresponding responsibilities for an MBA at your firm.

Our steady stream of investment activity is ideal for MBAs who want to put their talent to work immediately, with financings in a broad range of industries. Individual responsibilities are balanced with teamwork at every level, enabling associates to gain broad industry knowledge and market experience.

Specifically, private placement associates monitor portfolios with investments in about 25 companies, valued at about a half-billion dollars. Associates analyze industry trends, make on-site evaluations of potential investments, negotiate new deals, and present recommendations to senior management.

Public market associates evaluate market trends, research bond offerings, develop trading strategies, and present recommendations to senior managers responsible for multi-billion-dollar portfolios.

The Recruiting Process

Describe your recruiting process and the criteria by which you select candidates. Are grades a criterion? Is prior experience necessary?

TIAA Investments seeks talented MBAs majoring in finance to join our Securities Division. Superior communications skills and prior credit training and analysis experience at a major financial institution are strongly preferred. Along with quality investing, we emphasize teamwork and a balanced work and personal lifestyle.

A successful screening interview will be followed by an opportunity to meet with Securities officers and associates at our New York City headquarters.

We believe cultural and ethnic diversity is the lifeblood of a successful corporation, and this is reflected in our hiring record, our tradition of promoting from within, and our career development activities.

Toronto Dominion Bank

31 West 52nd Street
New York, NY 10019-6101
(212) 468-0638

MBA Recruiting Contact(s):
Daniel J. O'Connell, Assistant Manager
Human Resources

Company Description

Describe your firm's business and the types of clients served by your finance group(s).

Toronto Dominion Bank is a widely held, public corporation whose shares are listed on the Toronto, Montreal, and Tokyo Stock Exchanges. Total assets, as at January 31, 1993, were Cdn. $81.0 billion. TD is the fifth largest Canadian bank in terms of total assets and on the basis of common shareholders' equity.

Formally titled the Toronto-Dominion Bank, but usually referred to as TD Bank or simply TD, the bank was formed in 1955 through the merger of the Bank of Toronto (founded 1855) and the Dominion Bank (established 1869).

In Canada TD serves individuals, businesses, financial institutions, and governments through a network of over 900 branches from coast to coast. With the recent acquisition of Central Guaranty Trust, which is being merged into the TD's retail operations, the bank can now offer complete trust and fiduciary services in both the personal and business fields.

TD's corporate business is focused primarily on North America. In the United States and internationally, TD offers a broad range of credit and financial and advisory services to businesses, multinational corporations, governments, and correspondent banks through a network of offices in New York, Chicago, and Houston; London, Tokyo, Hong Kong, Singapore, and Taipei; and its Australian subsidiary in Melbourne.

A major strength of the TD is its financial position. In 1992, even though earnings declined, TD maintained its level of dividends and contributed $177 million to retained earnings, thereby further strengthening its capital base. TD has retained its position as one of the best-capitalized banks in the world, with one of the highest credit ratings of all major North American banks. Financial strength is a major advantage in tough times; custom-

ers may be drawn to a bank offering financial stability that also has the capital to invest in service, to pursue new strategies, and to take advantage of opportunities that arise.

Another strength is that TD, unlike its major competitors, has built, rather than bought, its own securities operation and offers integrated corporate and investment banking services. This provides the bank with an edge in its ability to react innovatively to shifting customer needs and changing economic times.

TD has a relatively flat, flexible organizational structure, which enables it to respond quickly and mobilize to meet new challenges, and it has been an innovative leader in many areas. Its discount brokerage is a prime example. Green Line Investor Services Inc. is now Canada's top discount broker, and it challenges all other brokerage houses for top spot in absolute number of trading orders on the Toronto Stock Exchange.

The bank is Canada's money market leader in key global derivatives niches.

By acquiring Central Guaranty Trust, TD was the first Canadian bank to take advantage of a new legislative climate and to move into the trust and fiduciary business in a major way. This variation from the bank's long-held policy of build rather than buy has catapulted it into a new and exciting challenge.

With its depth of experience in handling commercial paper in the corporate and business field, TD has also become the leader in Canada in distributing commercial paper to its individual customers.

In recent years there has been a significant shift away from interest income to fee income, and with its many noninterest products and services, TD has largely offset the decline in credit. The growth of such TD services as Private Placements, Fixed Income Issues, and Financial Advisory services have played a major role in this change, as have other relationship building services such as Payroll and Cash Management, of which there are many options available, enabling TD to service the largest to the smallest customers efficiently and profitably.

The Finance MBA's Job Description

Describe the career path and corresponding responsibilities for an MBA at your firm.

The Associate Development Program, a structured rotational program, gives a broad understanding of our business strategy, organization, and values; fundamental product knowledge and skills; and the professional contacts and visibility that help integrate an individual into the firm. Following formal orientation, MBAs rotate through Corporate Banking, Toronto Dominion Securities, Inc., Sales & Trading, and Special Industries (Communications Finance, Forest Products Finance, Health Care Finance, and Utilities Finance). After the program, Associates typically work in a group charged with researching, structuring, and negotiating transactions. Most individuals will experience several groups during their career with the bank.

The Recruiting Process

Describe your recruiting process and the criteria by which you select candidates. Are grades a criterion? Is prior experience necessary?

Toronto Dominion seeks MBAs who are focused on the financial services sector regardless of their work background. Successful candidates have strong analytical and selling skills, enjoy working in a team atmosphere, and exhibit initiative.

Do you have a summer program for associates? If so, please describe.

Summer interns work in a group on transactions and other analytical assignments as full members of the team. Through small group presentations, interns are exposed to all groups within the division. Each intern is evaluated at the end of the summer and receives consideration for the Associate Program.

United Airlines

P.O. Box 66100
Chicago, IL 60666
(708) 952-4000

MBA Recruiting Contact(s):
Jim Rynott, College Relations

Company Description

Describe your firm's business and the types of clients served by your finance group(s).

United Airlines is one of the largest international airlines in the world, with annual revenues in excess of $12 billion, more than 80,000 employees and a fleet of over 530 aircraft. Headquartered in Chicago, United Airlines flies to 169 airports in 33 countries on five continents. Domestically, it maintains key hubs at Washington, D.C., Chicago, Denver, and San Francisco.

Independent industry sources rank United Airlines as one of the U.S. "big three" in terms of size and other operating criteria. Much of the airline's recent focus has been expansion into the European community and the South American and Latin American marketplace. By the end of 1992, United had established the preeminent global route network of any airline.

Describe your ownership structure.

United Airlines is a publicly held company traded on the New York Stock Exchange, Midwest Stock Exchange, and the Pacific Stock Exchange under the symbol UAL.

A copy of UAL Corporation's annual report to the Securities and Exchange Commission on Form 10-K may be obtained from Investor Relations, UAL Corporation, (708) 952-7501.

The Finance MBA's Job Description

Describe the career path and corresponding responsibilities for an MBA at your firm.

MBAs who join United are initially assigned to positions in the Finance, Marketing, or Operations areas, providing a range of exposure to management issues and planning and looking for immediate contributions to the attainment of these goals. For financially oriented graduates, the emphasis is to use analytical tools to improve the airline's competitiveness in both operations and financial markets. The airline industry involves heavily leveraged assets. The goal is to maintain a balance sheet that gives management the freedom to pursue market opportunities competitively.

The Recruiting Process

Describe your recruiting process and the criteria by which you select candidates. Are grades a criterion? Is prior experience necessary?

United Airlines seeks highly motivated individuals who have the ability to work effectively with others. MBAs working at United possess diverse backgrounds and enjoy working in a fast-paced, project-oriented environment. The majority have two to three years of work experience prior to attending graduate school. Progression is analyst, senior analyst, manager, and director, based on a merit performance system.

Wasserstein Perella & Co.

31 West 52d Street
New York, NY 10019
(212) 969-2774

MBA Recruiting Contact(s):
Robert Pruzan, Vice President
(212) 969-2712

Company Description

Describe your firm's business and the types of clients served by your finance group(s).

Wasserstein Perella & Group Inc. is a leading international investment banking firm that is involved in three related lines of business: (1) advising a global base of clients on matters of corporate strategy, mergers, acquisitions, divestitures, and corporate finance; (2) specialized sales, trading, and research of debt and equity securities; and (3) management of investment funds and products that seek superior risk-adjusted returns for investors.

The firm is dedicated to providing superior client service and building long-term relationships. In pursuit of these goals, Wasserstein Perella quickly developed an international scope with a network that includes offices in New York, London, Paris, Frankfurt, Tokyo, Osaka, Chicago, Los Angeles, and Houston. Important to the firm's internationalization was its establishment in 1988 of an alliance with the Nomura Securities Co., Ltd., the world's largest securities firm. The firm has recruited the highest calibre of talent and now consists of over 150 professionals worldwide. Our 24 senior partners have more than 300 years in aggregate of industry experience.

To date, Wasserstein Perella has participated in many of the largest and most significant mergers and acquisitions in recent history and in some of the most innovative financings. The firm is equally proud of the many small divestitures and other transactions it has managed on behalf of its long-term clients and the numerous occasions when it has advised clients to forego transactions as a result of market or strategic factors. When providing corporate finance advice, clients turn to us as a sounding board to help choose among and implement the numerous financing alternatives Wall Street has to offer.

Wasserstein Perella's specialized sales, trading, and research activities are carried out through its wholly owned subsidiary, Wasserstein Perella Securities (WPS). Within WPS, the Grantchester Securities Division is one of the leading dealers of high-yield debt securities. Grantchester traded over $40 billion of high-yield securities over 1990–1992 and transacted business with 200 different institutions with varied investment profiles. The WPS Equity Division is a highly focused team that concentrates on the sales, trading, and research of selected equity securities. The recently created Emerging Capital Markets Division provides investor and corporate finance services for global investors in the Latin American, Eastern European, African, and Asian markets.

Wasserstein Perella has committed to building its asset management capabilities. The firm aims to have a strong presence in equity and fixed income money management of U.S. securities, selected international products, and an array of higher-return, higher-risk private investment funds. The cornerstone of this effort to date is the firm's $1.1 billion merchant banking fund.

Describe your ownership structure.

Wasserstein Perella is a privately owned corporation. Twenty percent of its equity is held by Nomura Securities, Ltd.

How does your approach to finance differ from that of other firms, and what do you consider to be your strengths and distinctive capabilities?

Wasserstein Perella offers custom-tailored mergers and acquisitions (M&A) and corporate finance solutions to meet clients' unique needs. The firm is known for its ability to solve complex financial and strategic problems. We are also viewed as an objective sounding board for financing decisions, and we are not prejudiced by a need to underwrite securities to cover the overhead of a large underwriting operation.

Discuss changes in your firm's revenues (both domestic and international) and professional staff over the past year; over the past five years.

We have had a gradual diversification of revenues away from domestic M&A toward high-yield and equity sales, trading and research, international M&A, privatizations, and asset management.

The Finance MBA's Job Description

Describe the career path and corresponding responsibilities for an MBA at your firm.

Associates are given responsibilities that are typically one year ahead of those at other investment banks. The typical time period between Associate and Vice President is three and a half years.

Describe the opportunities for professional mobility between the various departments in your firm.

Wasserstein Perella provides tremendous flexibility between departments and geographic locations.

Discuss the lifestyle aspects of a career with your firm (i.e., average hours per week, amount of travel, flexibility to change offices, corporate culture, etc.).

Lifestyle/culture is characterized as fun and entrepreneurial yet intense. Average hours per week are 60–70. Travel depends on the nature of projects. Associates usually travel 15–25% of their time.

The Recruiting Process

Describe your recruiting process and the criteria by which you select candidates. Are grades a criterion? Is prior experience necessary?

We usually conduct two-on-one on-campus interviews, followed by one or two visits to our New York office. Decisions are usually made quickly. We look for smart, energetic self-starters. Grades and previous experience are important factors.

In a typical year, how many permanent associates and analysts do you hire? Do you have a summer program for associates or analysts? If so, please describe.

Wasserstein Perella typically hires four to five Associates domestically and one to two internationally. We also hire three to four Summer Associates.

Wertheim Schroder & Co. Incorporated

787 Seventh Avenue
New York, NY 10019
(212) 492-6000

MBA Recruiting Contact(s):
Andrew J. Frankle, Associate—Investment Banking
(212) 492-6478

Company Description

Describe your firm's business and the types of clients served by your finance group(s).

Wertheim Schroder & Co. Incorporated, a privately held, major bracket investment banking firm founded in 1927, employs over 1,000 people worldwide, with offices in New York, Los Angeles, Houston, Boston, Philadelphia, Dallas, London, Paris, Geneva, and Amsterdam. The firm is actively involved in investment banking, sales and trading, arbitrage, securities research, and asset management.

In 1986, Schroders plc, the British merchant banking firm, purchased a 50% interest in Wertheim Schroder. The partnership with Schroders has served as the foundation for Wertheim Schroder to participate in the growing international financing and mergers and acquisitions markets. Schroders is one of the preeminent merchant banks in Europe and the Far East, with offices worldwide, including in London, Paris, Milan, Frankfurt, Madrid, Tokyo, Singapore, Hong Kong, and Sydney.

The Wertheim Schroder Investment Banking Department, consisting of approximately 70 professionals, is actively involved in all major areas of investment banking. Specific areas of expertise include mergers and acquisitions (M&A), both domestic and cross-border, public offerings of debt and equity securities, private placements of debt and equity securities, and bankruptcy reorganizations and financial restructurings. Wertheim Schroder provides investment banking services to companies in all industries. We have teams of investment banking and research professionals with particular expertise in the chemical, energy, industrial manufacturing, media and entertainment, health care, retailing, financial services, and transportation industries.

Wertheim Schroder is a leading financial advisor to U.S. and international companies in the structuring, execution, and financing of M&A. A particular strength of Wertheim Schroder's M&A practice is the exclusive sale of public and private companies, and their divisions and subsidiaries. The Wertheim/Schroder Group has consistently ranked in the top ten M&A advisors worldwide and was ranked third, with 80 transactions, in 1992.

Wertheim Schroder is a major bracket underwriter and an active manager of public equity offerings for its clients. In addition, Wertheim Schroder has extensive experience in private placements of debt and equity, and since 1987 has completed over 80 offerings with a value of over $5.5 billion. Wertheim Schroder is the market leader in U.S. dollar private placements for non-U.S. companies, and in 1992 ranked first among all investment banks in this area, completing approximately $1 billion of such financings.

Wertheim Schroder has had an exceptional record in recent years in merchant banking, particularly through investments in the chemicals, music publishing, and regional railroad industries. The firm has formed and manages a $250 million merchant banking fund to pursue additional investments. The fund's most recent investment was a sizable minority stake in Six Flags Theme Parks, Inc.

Describe your ownership structure.

Wertheim Schroder & Co. Incorporated is a privately owned company based in New York. The managing directors of Wertheim Schroder own 50% of the voting stock and control the management of the firm. Schroders plc, the leading British merchant bank, owns the remaining 50% of the voting stock of Wertheim Schroder. In order to expand the scope of its client base and develop new business alliances, in January 1990, Wertheim Schroder sold three strategic, nonvoting equity interests to Bank of Boston Corporation, a leading New England regional bank; Massachusetts Mutual Life Insurance Company, the twelfth largest insurance company in the United States; and Mitsubishi Trust and Banking Corporation, the largest trust company in the world.

The Finance MBA's Job Description

Wertheim Schroder offers its Associates the opportunities inherent in a growing international investment banking firm with the atmosphere of a traditional Wall Street partnership.

The role of an Associate in Wertheim Schroder's Investment Banking Department differs significantly from the role of an Associate in a larger investment bank. Associates are encouraged to obtain as broad experience as possible. Wertheim Schroder endeavors to ensure that all Associates obtain experience in all major areas of investment banking: general financial advisory, M&A, public and private placements of securities, bankruptcy reorganization and financial restructurings, and principal investments. Associates are also encouraged to become involved with clients in a diverse group of industries.

Because of the size and open structure of our department, Associates are encouraged to learn as much as possible and develop responsibility early. Rarely is a transaction or client serviced by more than three professionals or more than one Associate.

We believe that Wertheim Schroder offers a rare alternative to the aspiring investment banker who desires the breadth of experience and immediate responsibility of a growing yet highly sophisticated investment banking practice. At the same time, we believe that our collegial, relatively informal atmosphere creates a supportive environment for an Associate to develop his or her career.

The Recruiting Process

Describe your recruiting process and the criteria by which you select candidates. Are grades a criterion? Is prior experience necessary?

Wertheim Schroder interviews at the top MBA programs to find the small group of Associates it hires each year. Wertheim Schroder seeks highly motivated individuals with a record of business and academic achievement. Wertheim Schroder maintains a collegial atmosphere that supports initiative at all levels and seeks individuals who will succeed in this environment. Prior experience in finance or financial analysis is considered helpful but not required.

Do you have a summer program for associates or analysts? If so, please describe.

The firm does not have a summer program.

Weyerhaeuser Company

Tacoma, WA 98477
(206) 924-2367

MBA Recruiting Contact(s):
Robert C. Hirschey, Manager
Investment Evaluation Department

Company Description

Describe your firm's business and the types of clients served by your finance group(s).

Weyerhaeuser is the world's largest private owner of timber, a leader in commercial forest management, and one of North America's largest producers and exporters of forest products. Weyerhaeuser also has significant positions in U.S. real estate development and financial services operations.

Timber Growing and Harvesting

Weyerhaeuser Company owns about 5.8 million acres of timberland in the United States with a merchantable volume of over 8.6 billion cubic feet of timber, the largest of any other private owner. In addition to company-owned lands in the United States, the company has long-term harvest licenses on approximately 12 million acres of productive forest land in the Canadian provinces of British Columbia, Alberta, and Saskatchewan. The company also grows about 300,000 seedlings a year in company-owned seed orchards, greenhouses, and nurseries. Weyerhaeuser supports the management of these resources with the largest private silvicultural and environmental research staff in the world.

Weyerhaeuser Company is unique in the quality of its timber resource and forest management programs. The company began growing timber as a crop in the 1930s. In 1941 it publicly committed itself to sustainable yield forestry with the dedication of lands in southwestern Washington as a "Tree Farm," launching the national Tree Farm movement. The High Yield Forestry program was begun in 1966, which more than doubles annual growth per acre over unmanaged natural stands. These early decisions have provided a relatively stable raw material supply, making Weyerhaeuser less dependent on purchased timber and logs than other companies.

Wood Products Manufacturing

Weyerhaeuser is the world's largest producer of softwood lumber and the largest North American exporter of forest products. Weyerhaeuser manufactures a full range of wood products, including logs, lumber, chips, plywood, oriented strandboard, and composite products at 55 locations around the United States and Canada. The company markets and distributes these products through its own sales and distribution system to industrial, wholesale, and retail customers.

Pulp and Paper Manufacturing

Weyerhaeuser is a leading producer of pulp, newsprint, fine paper, containerboard and shipping containers, liquid packaging board, and chemicals, with 63 manufacturing sites located throughout the United States and Canada. Weyerhaeuser's Pulp Division is the world's largest supplier of market pulp. The Newsprint Division is the largest foreign supplier of newsprint to Japan. Pulp and paper products are marketed through Weyerhaeuser's own sales and marketing organization, as well as through merchant distributors. The company also operates one of the nation's largest wastepaper recycling businesses. Weyerhaeuser's Recycling Division is almost 20 years old and has grown rapidly to become one of the largest paper recyclers in the United States. The company now recycles approximately 1.7 million tons of wastepaper in 20 facilities.

Real Estate Development and Financial Services

Weyerhaeuser Real Estate Company (WRECO), a wholly owned subsidiary of Weyerhaeuser Company, engages in real estate development, residential and commercial building construction, and venture capital projects. These activities are conducted through several operating companies in California, Florida, Maryland, New Jersey, North Carolina, Texas, and Washington. WRECO is one of the largest home builders in the United States. Weyerhaeuser Mortgage Company is one of the nation's largest residential mortgage bankers, with 40 retail branch offices nationwide.

The Finance MBA's Job Description

Describe the career path and corresponding responsibilities for an MBA at your firm.

The Investment Evaluation Department (IED) is the preferred entry point for high-potential MBAs. IED is responsible for providing strategic, financial, and analytical leadership in all acquisition, divestiture, merger, joint venture, and new business evaluations. The group is also responsible for analyzing and forming independent judgments on Weyerhaeuser's major capital investment opportunities. IED is a small group within Weyerhaeuser's finance organization that deals substantially with the company's operating divisions, supporting major strategic and tactical decisions.

The Analyst position is the traditional entry point for the department. Analysts typically spend two to three years in IED gaining a broad perspective on Weyerhaeuser's businesses and exposure to senior corporate and operating level managers. The department's goal is to provide Analysts with a good general understanding of Weyerhaeuser businesses, as well as the opportunity to get to know many of the company's key managers in preparation for long-term careers in the company. The Department Project Directors and Manager provide guidance and advice as needed. The Analysts tend to move into a business unit of their choice, gaining experience in their areas of interest (marketing, finance, operations management, etc.) to lead them into general management positions.

Weyerhaeuser evaluates many proposals to expand or reconfigure its business groups. They include acquisition and joint venture opportunities within existing businesses, as well as in new business lines. They may also involve divestment or asset redeployment options aimed at upgrading Weyerhaeuser's existing portfolio of assets. The IED Analyst is a key member of the team evaluating an opportunity, with primary responsibility for performing the economic analysis. In many instances Analysts help develop the strategic framework for the opportunity. The Analyst must also ensure that the presentation of the proposal provides senior management with the key information needed to make the decision. After a decision has been reached, Analysts participate in the execution by drafting offering memorandums, working with investment bankers, coordinating buyers' due diligence, advising senior managers during negotiations, and evaluating alternative transaction structures.

Weyerhaeuser competes in highly capital-intensive industries and allocates significant capital resources to its existing businesses. IED brings conceptual and analytical leadership to the capital allocation effort. The analyst is primarily responsible for providing decision makers with independent, thorough, and timely economic analyses of diverse investment proposals. This is accomplished by working closely with business and operating groups, often on site. Some recent projects include the expansion of a joint venture newsprint operation with a Japanese partner, multistage modernizations and expansions at two Weyerhaeuser's largest pulp and paper complexes, and the reconfiguration of our southern sawmill capacity to align better with available raw material and product markets.

The Recruiting Process

Describe your recruiting process and the criteria by which you select candidates. Are grades a criterion? Is prior experience necessary?

IED is looking for MBAs who want to leverage their superior analytical ability, strong leadership, and interpersonal skills into a long-term general management career at Weyerhaeuser. New Analysts should have significant prior work experience, good business judgment, and a sense of perspective. They should also be comfortable working independently in a relatively unstructured environment.

In a typical year, how many permanent associates and analysts do you hire? Do you have a summer program for associates or analysts? If so, please describe.

IED hires one to three Analysts a year, primarily through recruiting at top MBA schools around the United States. There is no summer program.

Wheat, First Securities, Inc.

Wheat First Butcher Singer

901 East Byrd Street
Riverfront Plaza
Richmond, VA 23219

MBA Recruiting Contact(s):
Allen S. Morton, Managing Director
Karen W. Hughes, Recruiting Coordinator

Company Description

Describe your firm's business and the types of clients served by your finance group(s).

Wheat, First Securities, Inc. is a full-service securities firm that serves primarily the mid-Atlantic and Southeast regions of the United States. Founded in 1934, Wheat employs approximately 2,000 people, including 750 retail financial consultants, in 92 regional offices located in 12 states. The firm is owned entirely by its management and an employee stock ownership plan. Wheat provides comprehensive securities brokerage, investment banking, and other financial services to individuals and institutional investors, corporations, municipalities, and government agencies. The firm employs its own capital resources to trade and underwrite securities.

Wheat is considered a leading regional investment bank in its core businesses: equity, municipal and corporate debt underwriting, and merger and acquisition advisory services. Wheat's Municipal Finance Group was ranked the number one non–New York firm on the East Coast for 1992. This group led or comanaged more than $2.25 billion in 1992, more than double the performance in 1991. Wheat's Corporate Finance Group underwrote $2.1 billion in equity and debt in 1992. Wheat's Financial Institutions Group in Corporate Finance ranked number one in capital raised in 1992 out of all non–New York investment banks.

Wheat is organized into three primary groups: the Capital Markets Group, the Private Client Group, and the Asset Management Group. The Capital Markets Group encompasses Investment Banking Services, including equity and debt underwriting of public and private securities and merger and acquisition advisory services. Municipal Finance and Taxable Fixed Income are also part of Capital Markets. The Private Client Group encompasses all of Wheat's 92 retail branch locations and Fully Disclosed Clearing Services. The Asset Management Group contains Wheat Funds, including Commonwealth Investment Counsel, Charter Asset Management, and Cambridge Advisors.

Discuss changes in your firm's revenues (both domestic and international) and professional staff over the past year; over the past five years.

Wheat's revenues have grown dramatically in recent years. Revenues increased from $70 million in 1985 to $311 million for the fiscal year ended March 31, 1993. Revenue growth from fiscal 1992 to 1993 was 20%.

The Finance MBA's Job Description

Describe the career path and corresponding responsibilities for an MBA at your firm.

Upon arriving at Wheat, new investment banking associates begin a training program that consists primarily of on-the-job-type projects and secondarily of group sessions led by internal and external professionals, that address various finance, accounting, and legal issues. Typically, investment banking associates spend their early years working with a variety of industry groups, senior professionals, and transaction types in an effort to broaden their career development and corporate finance skills. Associates eventually focus their efforts on a specific industry. The goal is to expose associates to a rich variety of assignments and level of client responsibility.

The Recruiting Process

Describe your recruiting process and the criteria by which you select candidates. Are grades a criterion? Is prior experience necessary?

Wheat seeks highly motivated individuals with a demonstrated record of achievement who have the ability to work effectively with clients and other professionals in the firm. Wheat investment bankers have a diverse background. Common characteristics of Wheat associates include strong initiative, ability to relate well to clients and other professionals, a team-oriented attitude, a strong work ethic, and excellent analytical and communication skills. Corporate Finance associates typically have prior investment banking experience before coming to Wheat.

In a typical year, how many associates and analysts do you hire? Do you have a summer program for associates or analysts? If so, please describe.

The number of associates hired each year depends on Wheat's internal needs.

Wheat's Summer Associate program gives students finishing their first year of business school an opportunity to learn about Wheat and its various departments while participating in corporate finance projects and transactions that span industry groups and transaction types. The number of summer associates hired in a particular summer depends upon the demands of the marketplace and Wheat's hiring outlook.

The World Bank Group

1818 H Street, NW
Washington, DC 20433

MBA Recruiting Contact(s):
Aloysius Ordu, Administrator
Young Professionals Program

Company Description

Describe your firm's business and the types of clients served by your finance group(s).

The World Bank Group is the world's largest agency for economic development. Its overriding aim is to help raise the standards of living in developing countries by channeling financial resources from developed countries.

In pursuit of a broad agenda that has evolved, the Bank Group has made loans totaling more than $245 billion over nearly 50 years. Reducing poverty in developing countries remains at the core of that agenda, which also includes promoting sound environmental policies and helping Eastern and Central European countries make the transition to market-oriented economies.

The World Bank Group is a multilateral lending agency consisting of four closely associated institutions:

> International Bank for Reconstruction and Development (IBRD)
> International Development Association (IDA)
> International Finance Corporation (IFC)
> Multilateral Investment Guarantee Agency (MIGA)

It is owned by more than 150 member governments. Voting power is linked to capital subscriptions, which are based on each country's relative economic strength. The IBRD obtains most of its funds through the sale of bonds.

Ask, "What is the World Bank Group?" in newly industrialized countries, such as Brazil and the Republic of Korea, and the answer is likely to be the International Bank for Reconstruction and Development. The IBRD makes market rate loans, amounting to about $15 billion a year, and provides training and technical advice to help developing countries address their own problems.

Ask the same question of poorer developing countries, such as Bangladesh, Ghana, and Haiti, with per capita incomes below $500 a year, and the answer is likely to be the International Development Association. IDA provides these countries with interest-free loans of about $5 billion each year, along with training and technical advice.

Ask entrepreneurs eager to build a cement factory in India or a hotel in the Caribbean, and the answer is the International Finance Corporation. Working with investors around the world, the IFC mobilizes capital for promising private ventures held back by inadequate financing. The IFC approved investments in 1992 totaling $1.8 billion for 167 projects, with total estimated costs of $12 billion. The IFC also approved $1.4 billion in syndicated loans and in underwriting.

The Multilateral Investment Guarantee Agency (MIGA) was established in April 1988 to promote the flow of foreign direct investment by insuring investments against noncommercial (political) risk and to provide promotional and advisory services to help countries create an attractive investment climate.

Most people around the world think of the World Bank Group as a supplier of funds. But on New York's Wall Street, Tokyo's Kabuto-Cho, or in London's financial district, the Bank is thought of as one of the world's largest borrowers—and as a borrower with a triple-A credit rating.

The Finance MBA's Job Description

Describe the career path and corresponding responsibilities for an MBA at your firm.

The Young Professionals Program is a starting point for careers in the World Bank Group. The program is designed for highly qualified and motivated young people skilled in economics, finance, or a technical field relevant to the Bank Group's operations. The program provides the opportunity for professional development through on-the-job experience and exposure to the Bank Group's operations and policies.

Young Professionals start with two six-month rotational assignments in different departments—experiences that provide a broad overview of the Bank Group's work. Treated as full-fledged staff members with specific responsibilities, the Young Professionals are expected to make significant contributions to the work programs of their departments. Each rotational assignment normally involves at least one field mission.

The choice of a Young Professional's assignments is based on qualifications, personal preferences, and institutional staffing needs. Like all other staff, Young Professionals are on probation for at least one year, and they can apply to a confirmed position upon successful completion of their rotational assignments.

The World Bank Group offers a wide selection of career paths to Young Professionals. They are encouraged to move from complex to complex (including IFC) and specialty to specialty over the course of their careers.

Young Professionals who choose permanent assignments in operations can expect to take on task management responsibilities soon after joining the Bank—managing multimillion dollar loans and credits and the human, financial, and technical resources that go into them.

There is no typical career path for a Young Professional. Former Young Professionals work throughout the organization in a variety of staff and managerial positions.

The Recruiting Process

Describe your recruiting process and the criteria by which you select candidates. Are grades a criterion? Is prior experience necessary?

Competition is intense, with about 3,500 applications received for each year's 30–40 positions. Because most preliminary and final candidates meet or exceed the hiring criteria, selection is extremely difficult.

Candidates must have a master's degree (or equivalent) in economics, finance, or a technical field relevant to the Bank Group's operations, plus a minimum of two years of relevant work experience or academic study at the doctoral level. All candidates are expected to have superior academic records and must be less than 32 years of age.

Fluency in English is required, and speaking proficiency in one or more of the Bank Group's other working languages—Arabic, Chinese, French, Portuguese, Russian, and Spanish—is a plus. Work experience in a developing country is a strength.

The application deadline is each October 31, with final selections made the following March. Since we conduct on- and off-campus discussions early each fall, we encourage candidates to contact us well in advance of that date.

Candidates who do not qualify for the Young Professionals Program due to age or specialization and are interested in the World Bank may apply directly to the Recruitment Division.

In a typical year, how many permanent associates and analysts do you hire? Do you have a summer program for associates or analysts? If so, please describe.

Each year, 30–40 candidates are accepted into the Young Professionals Program.

The World Bank offers summer employment to about 150 students from universities worldwide. Candidates must have at least a bachelor's degree and must be full-time, degree-seeking students in both spring and fall semesters of the year they would like to work, pursuing at least a master's degree. The majority of the vacancies, although they vary from year to year, require training in economics, finance, accounting, or statistics, combined with computer skills, several months of relevant work experience, and familiarity with one or more languages other than English. Some positions require backgrounds in agriculture, environment, information systems, social sciences, and law. Interested students should contact the Summer Employment Program in December. The IFC administers a separate Summer Employment Program.

Glossary

Excerpted from Doing Deals: Investment Banks at Work by *Robert G. Eccles and Dwight B. Crane (Boston: Harvard Business School Press, 1988). The following terms and definitions are intended to explain terms used in* Doing Deals *and do not necessarily cover all possible meanings of the terms.*

Arbitrage: occurs when there is an opportunity to buy one security and sell another security and make a riskless profit. An arbitrage opportunity exists when two securities are mispriced relative to each other, so that it is possible to buy one and sell the other and make a risk-free profit. In the investment banking context, the term *arbitrage* is often used to refer to an activity when an acquisition is announced at a higher price than the current stock price of the target firm. The risk arbitrage department of an investment bank then decides whether to buy the stock to take advantage of the higher offer price.

Asset-Backed Securities: a security backed by a pool of assets, such as automobile loans. The cash flow from the pool of assets is used to make interest and principal payments on the securities.

Asset Valuations: usually refers to the valuation of assets in a merger and acquisition transaction. An investment bank is asked to estimate the value of the various parts of the firm that might be acquired.

Block Trading: trading of a large quantity of securities. The New York Stock Exchange considers a block trade to be equal to ten thousand or more shares.

Bond: see **Debt.**

Bought Deal: in securities underwriting, a firm commitment to purchase an entire issue outright from the issuing company. In recent years this term has been used to mean a firm commitment by one or a small number of investment banking firms.

Boutique: a small, specialized securities firm that deals with a limited clientele and offers a limited product line . . . [e.g.,] with advisory services for issuers.

Bridge Loan: a short-term loan made by an investment bank to facilitate a transaction. It is made in anticipation of a security issue that would repay the loan.

Call Date: the date on which issuers have the right to call in or redeem outstanding bonds before their scheduled maturity.

Capital Markets Desk: a group of investment bankers who typically sit on the trading floor. They provide a direct link between issuing customers and the market.

Collaterized Mortgage Obligation (CMO): a security backed by mortgage bonds. The cash flows from the mortgage bonds are typically separated into different portions (e.g., they can be separated into short-, intermediate-, and long-term portions of the mortgages). Each class is paid a fixed rate of interest at regular intervals.

Co-Manager: works with a lead manager and often a group of other co-managers to manage a security underwriting.

Commercial Paper: a short-term debt with maturities ranging from 2 to 270 days, issued by corporations and other short-term borrowers.

Common Stock: a security representing ownership in a public corporation. Owners are entitled to vote on the selection of directors and other corporate matters. They typically receive dividends on their holdings, but corporations are not required to pay dividends. In the event that a corporation is liquidated, the claims of creditors and preferred stockholders take precedence over the claims of those who own common stock.

Convertible Bond: a bond that can be exchanged for a specified number of shares of common stock.

Credit Rating: typically refers to bond and commercial paper ratings assigned by Standard & Poor's, Moody's, or other credit-rating agencies.

Debt: a security that indicates a legal obligation to a borrower to repay principal and interest on specified dates. It is a general name for bonds, notes, mortgages, and other forms of credit obligations.

Distribution: the sale of a new security issue to investors.

Divestiture: the sale of a corporate asset such as a division.

Due Diligence: a process investment banks undertake to assure that information provided in a security offering is accurate.

Earnings per Share (EPS): the net income of a corporation divided by the number of shares outstanding.

116

Equity: represents ownership in a public corporation as evidenced by holding of common stock or preferred stock.

Eurobond: bond denominated in U.S. dollars or other currencies and sold to investors outside the country whose currency is used (e.g., a U.S. corporation could issue U.S. dollar-denominated securities to European investors.

Fixed-Income Security: a security that pays a fixed rate of return, such as a fixed rate of interest on a corporate bond.

Floating-Rate Debt: a security with interest payments that vary or "float" in response to prevailing interest rates, such as U.S. Treasuries.

Full-Service Firm: an investment bank that offers a wide range of financial services. The term is also used to refer to securities firms that have both extensive retail brokerage and investment banking services for large institutions.

Hedge: an investment strategy used to reduce risk. It typically involves the purchase or sale of contracts designed to offset the change in value of another security.

Hostile Takeover: an acquisition that takes place against the wishes of the management and board of directors of the target company.

Initial Public Offering (IPO): a corporation's first offering of common stock to the public.

Institutional Investor: an organization that holds and trades large volumes of securities such as pension funds, life insurance companies, and mutual funds.

International Bond: a bond issued outside the home country of the borrowing entity. International bonds can be subdivided into Eurobonds and foreign bonds. Foreign bonds are bonds sold primarily in the country of the currency of the issue.

Investment-Grade Bond: typically regarded as a bond with a credit rating of A or better.

Junk Bond: see **Noninvestment-Grade Bond.**

Lead Manager: works with a group of co-managers to form a syndicate to underwrite a security issue. A lead manager normally "runs the books" (manages the underwriting and determines distribution allocation) and is usually the investment bank that originated the deal.

League Table Rankings: published in various trade magazines that rank security underwriters by the volume of securities underwritten.

Lease: a contract granting use of real estate, equipment, or other fixed assets for a specified period of time in exchange for a series of payments.

Leveraged Buyout (LBO): the purchase of a company, or part of a company, using borrowed funds. The target company's assets frequently serve as security for the loans taken out by the acquiring firm. These loans are then repaid out of the acquired company's cash flow.

Make a Market: trading a security in order to provide liquidity and market prices to investors.

Master Limited Partnership: a limited partnership compromises a general partner, who manages a project and limited partners, who invest money but have limited liability. Frequently, limited partnerships are found in real estate and in oil and gas. A master limited partnership is a limited partnership that is publicly traded to give the investors liquidity.

Merchant Banking: in the context of U.S. investment banking, *merchant banking* refers to activities in which the firm commits its own capital to a transaction, as it does with bridge loans or when it makes equity investments in a company.

Mergers and Acquisitions (M&A): a general term that refers to various combinations of companies. A merger occurs when two or more companies combine; an acquisition occurs when one company takes over a controlling interest in another. M&A groups in investment banks work on these transactions, and they also advise on other kinds of related transactions, such as divestitures and repurchase of significant amounts of corporate stock.

Money-Market Paper: a short-term instrument such as commercial paper that is purchased by corporations and institutions that hold short-term liquid investment portfolios.

Money-Market Preferred Stock: a preferred stock instrument that has been structured to appeal to short-term investors such as investors that purchase regular money-market paper. The preferred stock is repriced every forty-nine days so that it trades like an instrument with a forty-nine-day maturity. From the point of view of the buyer, the advantage of preferred stock is that corporate holders of preferred and other stock only pay income tax on 15 percent of the dividend.

Mortgage-Backed Security: a security backed by a pool of mortgages. The cash flow from the pool of mortgages is used to make interest and principal payments on the security.

Noninvestment-Grade Bonds: technically, bonds with credit ratings of less than A. They are typically issued by companies without a long track record of sales and earnings or by companies that have experienced difficulty and have questionable credit strength. These securities are often used as a means to finance takeovers.

Origination: obtaining a mandate from an issuer to manage the underwriting and distribution of a new security issue.

Preferred Stock: a class of security that lies somewhere between bonds and common stock. Like interest on debt, dividends are paid on preferred stock at a specified rate, and holders of preferred stock take precedence over holders of common stock in the payment of dividends and liquidation of assets. Creditors, however, are ahead of preferred stockholders in the event of liquidation, and the company does not have a legal obligation to pay preferred stock dividends. Most preferred stock is cumulative, so that if the dividends are not paid for any reason, they accumulate and must be paid before dividends are paid to common stockholders.

Preliminary Prospectus: the first document released by an underwriter describing a new issue to prospective investors. It offers financial details about the issue but does not contain all of the information that will appear in the final prospectus. Portions of the cover page of the preliminary prospectus are printed in red ink, so it is popularly called a red herring.

Primary Market: the first time a security is sold to investors.

Private Placement: securities that are directly placed with an institutional investor, such as an insurance company, rather than sold through a public issue. Private placements do not have to be registered with the Securities and Exchange Commission, so these placements can occur more rapidly and with less information made available to the public.

Recapitalization: a change in a corporation's capital structure such as when the corporation exchanges bonds for outstanding stock. Some companies have been recapitalized in this fashion to make them less attractive targets for takeover.

Refinancing: when outstanding bonds are retired by using proceeds from the issuance of new securities. Refinancings are undertaken to reduce the interest rate or to otherwise improve the terms of the outstanding debt.

Restrictive Covenants: terms in a debt agreement that are designed to protect the creditor's interests. Covenants normally cover such matters as minimum amounts of working capital, maximum debt-equity ratios, and limits on dividend payments.

Retail Distribution: the capability of a securities firm to distribute securities to individual investors through retail brokers.

Secondary Trading: trading of securities which have already been issued in the primary marketplace. Thus, proceeds of secondary-market sales accrue to selling dealers and investors, not to the companies that originally issued the securities.

Securities and Exchange Commission (SEC): the federal agency created by the Securities Exchange Act of 1934 to administer that act and the Securities Act of 1933. The SEC is made up of five commissioners, appointed by the president. The statutes they administer are designed to promote full public disclosure and protect the investing public against malpractice in the securities markets. All issues of securities in the United States must be registered with the SEC.

Shelf Registration (Rule 415): a rule adopted by the SEC in 1982 that allows a corporation to preregister a public offering of securities. That is, they can preregister for up to two years prior to a public offering of securities. Once the security has been registered it is "on the shelf" and the company can go to market with the security as conditions become favorable.

Special Bracket Firm: an investment banking firm that leads the bulk of securities underwritten in the United States. The six special bracket firms [in 1987] are First Boston; Goldman, Sachs; Merrill Lynch; Morgan Stanley; Salomon Brothers; and Shearson Lehman Brothers.

Swap: has two meanings in the context of the securities markets. First, *swap* refers to the act of swapping from one type of security to another, such as an investor who swaps out of bonds into equities. Second, in a more recent use of the word, *swap* refers to debt obligations that are swapped between two borrowers (e.g., a borrower with floating-rate debt may swap its interest payment obligations with a borrower of fixed-rate debt; thus, the floating-rate debt issuer converts its debt into a fixed rate obligation).

Syndicate: a group of investment banks that agree to purchase a new issue of securities from an issuer for resale to the investment public. These investment banks agree to underwrite the securities. That is, they guarantee to purchase the securities. This group of banking firms is normally part of the selling group that distributes the security to the ultimate investors.

Syndicate Desk: coordinates the underwriting function of an investment bank. It helps price the security, works with the other members of the syndicate, and determines the allocation between retail and institutional investors.

Tax-Exempt Bond: a bond whose interest is exempt from taxation by federal, state, or local authorities. It is frequently called a municipal bond even though it may have been issued by a state government or agency or by an entity that is not a municipality. General obligation bonds are backed by the full faith and credit of the issuing entity. These bonds may be underwritten by commercial banks as well as by investment banks. Revenue bonds are backed by the anticipated revenues of the issuing authority. Under present legislation, commercial banks may not underwrite revenue bonds.

Tender Offer: an offer to buy shares of a corporation for cash or securities, or both, often with the objective of taking control of a target company. The Securities and Exchange Commission requires a corporate investor accumulating 5 percent or more of a target company to disclose the investment.

Thrift Institution: the major forms of thrift institutions are savings and loans and savings banks. These and other organizations receive consumer savings deposits and invest most of their assets in residential mortgages.

Tombstone: an advertisement placed in newspapers and magazines by investment bankers to announce an offering of securities. It gives basic details about the issue and lists the underwriting group members in a manner that indicates the relative size of their participation.

Underwrite: securities firms underwrite a securities issue by assuming the risk of buying the issue and then reselling the securities to the public either directly or through dealers.

U.S. Treasuries: securities issued by the federal government to borrow money.

Wirehouse: a national or international brokerage firm that has a large retail network of branch offices.

1994 Finance Career Guide Questionnaire

Company Description

Describe your firm's business and the types of clients served by your finance group(s).

Describe your ownership structure.

How does your approach to finance differ from that of other firms, and what do you consider to be your strengths and distinctive capabilities?

Discuss changes in your firm's revenues (both domestic and international) and professional staff over the past year; over the past five years.

The Finance MBA's Job Description

Describe the career path and corresponding responsibilities for an MBA at your firm.

Describe the opportunities for professional mobility between the various departments in your firm.

Discuss the lifestyle aspects of a career with your firm (i.e., average hours per week, amount of travel, flexibility to change offices, corporate culture, etc.).

The Recruiting Process

Describe your recruiting process and the criteria by which you select candidates. Are grades a criterion? Is prior experience necessary?

In a typical year, how many permanent associates and analysts do you hire? Do you have a summer program for associates or analysts? If so, please describe.

What international opportunities does your firm offer for U.S. citizens? For foreign nationals?

Mailing List

This is a mailing list of the firms profiled in the *Harvard Business School Career Guide: Finance, 1994*. Entries are arranged alphabetically and contain the name of the firm, address, phone number, and MBA recruiting contact. Some entries contain alternate contacts. Please refer to the company profile to see if another contact would be more appropriate for you. Before sending letters to the firms on the list, always call to verify the address and the name of the recruiting contact. Firms can move their headquarters, and people do change jobs.

Lester H. Krone
A.G. Edwards & Sons, Inc.
One North Jefferson
St. Louis, MO 63103
(314) 289-3000

Deborah Barry
Bankers Trust
280 Park Avenue 32W
New York, NY 10017
(212) 454-1767

William E. Mills
(212) 272-3506
Bear Stearns & Co. Inc.
245 Park Avenue
New York, NY 10167
(212) 272-2000

Patricia B. Davis
Vice President
BNY Associates
60 State Street
Boston, MA 02109
(617) 573-9100

Robert G. Calton III
Bowles Hollowell Conner & Co.
227 West Trade Street
Charlotte, NC 28202
(704) 348-1000

George Carbone
Managing Associate
Broadview Associates, L.P.
One Bridge Plaza
Fort Lee, NJ 07024
(201) 346-9000

Allan B. Wechsler
Personnel Manager
Brown Brothers Harriman & Co.
59 Wall Street
New York, NY 10005
(212) 483-1818

Mike Armstrong
Director
Burns Fry Limited
1 First Canadian Place
Suite 5000
P.O. Box 150
Toronto, Ontario M5X 1H3
Canada
(416) 359-4000

Craig S. Isom
Supervisor
Finance MBA Development Program
Chevron Corporation
225 Bush Street
San Francisco, CA 94104-4289
(415) 894-2752

J. Morton Davis
Chairman
D.H. Blair Investment Banking Corp.
44 Wall Street
New York, NY 10005
(212) 495-4000

Andrea B. Byrnes
Vice President
Donaldson, Lufkin & Jenrette
140 Broadway
New York, NY 10005
(212) 504-3000

Lucy Marshall
MBA Recruiting Coordinator
Enron Gas Services Corporation
1400 Smith Street
Houston, TX 77002
(713) 853-6614

FMC College Relations Corporation
200 East Randolph Drive
Chicago, IL 60601

Maryann K. Noonan
MBA Recruiting—Investment Banking
The First Boston Corporation
Park Avenue Plaza
New York, NY 10055
(212) 909-2000

Jeff Hitchcock
Ford Motor Company
20000 Rotunda Drive
P.O. Box 2053
Scientific Research Lab
Dearborn, MI 48121
(313) 845-5366

Nick Hotchkin
General Motors Corporation
New York Treasurer's Office
GM Building
767 Fifth Avenue
New York, NY 10153
(212) 418-6193

David M. Darst
Vice President—Equities Division
Goldman, Sachs & Co.
85 Broad Street
New York, NY 10004
(212) 902-1000

George Chung
Hewlett-Packard Company
175 Wyman Street
Waltham, MA 02254
(617) 290-3025

Ralph E. Barisano
IBM Corporation
One Copley Place
Boston, MA 02116
(617) 638-1907

Cornelis de Kievit
Manager, Recruitment
The International Finance Corporation
1818 H Street, NW
Room I-2193
Washington, DC 20433
(202) 473-7972

Jennifer Kovetz
J. & W. Seligman & Co., Incorporated
130 Liberty Street
New York, NY 10006
(212) 488-0281

Andrea Beldecos
Vice President, Corporate Finance Recruiting
J.P. Morgan & Co.
60 Wall Street
New York, NY 10260
(212) 483-2323

Carlo Bronzini
Associate
James D. Wolfensohn Incorporated
599 Lexington Avenue
New York, NY 10022
(212) 909-8100

Linda Bushlow
Vice President, Investment Banking
Joseph Luciano
Vice President, Research and Asset Management
Michael Burbank
Senior Vice President, Investment Services
(Retail Brokerage)
Kidder, Peabody & Co. Incorporated
10 Hanover Square
New York, NY 10005
(212) 510-3000

Rita Haring
Investment Banking
Lehman Brothers
American Express Tower
World Financial Center
New York, NY 10285
(212) 298-2000

John W. Rae, Jr.
Director, Recruiting and Training
Merrill Lynch & Co. Inc.
World Financial Center
250 Vesey Street
New York, NY 10281-1331
(212) 449-9836

Sharon Henning
Vice President
Montgomery Securities
600 Montgomery Street
San Francisco, CA 94111
(415) 627-2000

Patricia Palumbo
Morgan Stanley & Co. Incorporated
1251 Avenue of the Americas
New York, NY 10020
(212) 703-8482

Mark Brown
Manager, College Recruiting
NationsBank
NationsBank Corporate Center
NC1-007-2108
Charlotte, NC 28255
(704) 386-8200

Ariel Kochi
Vice President
Nomura Securities International, Inc.
2 World Financial Center
Building B
New York, NY 10281
(212) 667-9237

Mark Copman
Vice President
Piper Jaffray Inc.
222 South Ninth Street
Minneapolis, MN 55402
(612) 342-6000

Gary A. Downing
Managing Director, Corporate Finance
Raymond James & Associates, Inc.
800 Carillon Parkway
St. Petersburg, FL 33716
(813) 573-3800

R. Jamie Anderson
Vice President and Director
RBC Dominion Securities Inc.
P.O. Box 21
Commerce Court South
Toronto, Ontario M5L 1A7
Canada
(416) 864-3932

Ed McCrady
Vice President
The Robinson-Humphrey Company, Inc.
Atlanta Financial Center
3333 Peachtree Road, NE
Atlanta, GA 30326
(404) 266-6000

Gregory A. Milavsky
Vice President
Rothschild Canada Limited
1 First Canadian Place
Suite 3800
P.O. Box 77
Toronto, Ontario M5X 1B1
Canada
(416) 369-9600

Stephanie C. Flack
Vice President, Director of Human Resources
S.G. Warburg & Co. Inc.
787 Seventh Avenue
New York, NY 10019
(212) 459-7728

Christine A. Simpson
Vice President, Investment Banking Recruiting
Salomon Brothers Inc
Seven World Trade Center
New York, NY 10048
(212) 783-7000

Matthew R. Simmons
President
Simmons & Company International
700 Louisiana
Suite 4900
Houston, TX 77002
(713) 236-9999

Basil A. Bliss
Vice President
Smith Barney, Harris Upham & Co. Incorporated
1345 Avenue of the Americas
New York, NY 10105
(212) 698-3601

Robert A. Moll
Human Resources Officer
Teachers Insurance and Annuity Association-College Retirement Equities Fund (TIAA-CREF)
730 Third Avenue
New York, NY 10017

Daniel J. O'Connell
Assistant Manager, Human Resources
Toronto Dominion Bank
31 West 52d Street
New York, NY 10019-6101
(212) 468-0638

Jim Rynott
College Relations
United Airlines
P.O. Box 66100
Chicago, IL 60666
(708) 952-4000

Robert Pruzan
Vice President
Wasserstein Perella & Co.
31 West 52d Street
New York, NY 10019
(212) 969-2774

Andrew J. Frankle
Associate—Investment Banking
Wertheim Schroder & Co. Incorporated
787 Seventh Avenue
New York, NY 10019
(212) 492-6000

Robert C. Hirschey
Manager, Investment Evaluation Department
Weyerhaeuser Company
Tacoma, WA 98477
(206) 924-2367

Allen S. Morton
Managing Director
Wheat, First Securities, Inc.
901 East Byrd Street
Riverfront Plaza
Richmond, VA 23219

Aloysius Ordu
Administrator, Young Professionals Program
The World Bank Group
1818 H Street, NW
Washington, DC 20433

Selective Bibliography on the Finance Industry

Directories

Association for Investment Management and Research: Membership Directory. Charlottesville, VA: The Association. Main listings by Societies, data include member firm, special qualifications, fields of research, industry and functional specialities, primary Society membership, and designation for members that are CFAs. Alphabetic index by member name. AIMR information includes historical information, officers, awards, recipients, and Code of Ethics and Standards of Professional Conduct, etc. Annual.

Cary, Lucis. *The Venture Report Guide to Venture Capital in Europe.* 5th ed. London: Pitman, 1991. Heavy concentration of U.K. firms, information includes firm history, sources of funds, fees, decision-making process, key management, and profiles of investments. Included is a listing of EVCA members and indexes of investees and of providers.

Corporate Finance: The IDD Review of Investment Banking. New York: IDD, Inc. Reviews all public offerings completed in the United States, broken out by type of security, underwriter, and a comprehensive listing of the terms of deals done. Organized by issuer, data include U.S. issuers in the U.S. domestic market; excluded are debt-for-debt equity swaps, best efforts deals, private placements, and overallotments. Semiannual.

The Corporate Finance Bluebook. New York: Zehring Publications. Focuses on financial decision-making personnel at 5,000 public and private firms. U.S. parent and major U.S.-based subsidiaries of foreign parent companies included hold the 2,000 largest corporate pension funds. For each firm, sales and employee size; exchange; SICs; description of business; computer system hardware; officers; outside firms providing services; personnel and area of responsibility. Indexes. Annual companion to *The Corporate Financial Sourcebook.*

The Corporate Financial Sourcebook. New York: Zehring Publications. Nineteen types of capital funding and management firms, including venture capitalists, major private lenders, commercial financiers and factors, lessors, commercial and investment banks, intermediaries, pensions managers, master trusts, cash managers, corporate and real estate services, business insurance brokers, and CPAs. Data about firms vary according to types of activity. Over 3,600 firms and 20,000 executives are included. Annual companion to *The Corporate Finance Bluebook.*

Directory of Buyout Financing Sources. New York: SDC Publishing. Detailed profiles of more than 500 firms worldwide that provide debt and equity financing for buyouts. Arranged alphabetically within U.S. and foreign sections, information includes addresses, principals, services offered, and the types of transactions. Indexes include a list of leveraged buyout professionals, industry preferences, and companies. The emphasis is on U.S. firms.

Directory of M&A Intermediaries. New York: SDC Publishing. Five hundred and seventy-one investment banks, business brokers, law firms, and their intermediaries in the world. Also contains articles on mergers and acquisitions and leveraged buyouts. The U.S. listing is by state; foreign firms are entered alphabetically. Entries include name and title; type of firm; affiliation; services offered; percentage of intermediary work and other financial services; transaction, geographic and industry preferences; and types of principal clients. Indexes are by industry preference, professionals, and areas of international activities. Annual companion to *The Directory of Buyout Financing Sources.*

Directory of Pension Funds and Their Investment Managers. Charlottesville, VA: Money Market Directories. Companies included have a minimum of $7 million in total employee benefit fund assets; unions, governments, endowments, and foundations each hold more than $1 million in tax-exempt assets. Listings are geographic and include funds, managers, offices, and asset allocations. Indexes list asset rankings, managers by firms, officers, investment style/strategy, and major clients. Accompanied by *Money Market Directory of Pension Funds: Northeast Edition.* Annual, with updates.

The Guide to Venture Capital in Asia. Hong Kong: Asian Venture Capital Journal Limited. Similar in format to *Pratt's*, the guide's sections include a history and prospective of venture capital in the Asia Pacific region; details of the industry by country; and profiles of 220 venture capital firms operating in Asia. Indexes include a multilingual glossary and a listing of venture capital-backed initial public offerings. Annual.

National Association of Real Estate Investment Trusts. *Directory of Members.* Washington, DC: The Association. Alphabetical listing by firm, giving trustees, types of investment, assets, liabilities and equity statistics, and stock range. Semiannual.

Nelson's Directory of Investment Managers. Port Chester NY: Nelson Publications. Seventeen hundred investment management firms profiled, including executives, organizational overviews, specialties, assets managed, clients, decision-making process, fees, and holdings. Indexes by geography, total assets managed, investment managers by organization, type of investment, specialties, and products offered. Annual.

Pratt's Guide to Venture Capital Sources. Wellesley Hills, MA: Venture Economics, Inc. Signed articles on venture capitalism, sources of financing and business development, and going public. The major index is a geographic listing of U.S. venture capital firms (contact persons, type of firm; type of financing; annual sales; geographic, industry, and project preferences). Separate section of foreign venture capital companies is an expansion of the Canadian indexes, reflecting the growing globalization of venture capital. Annual.

The Real Estate Directory of Major Investors: Developers and Brokers. Wilmette, IL: Reed Business Publishing (USA). Contains 3,000 companies and institutions: major national and international investors, brokers and developers of income-producing property (minimum investment $1 million). Primary index is alphabetical by firm (employee size, key personnel, geographic preferences, average purchase price/investment range per property); additional indexes are by geographic locations, geographic preferences, and personnel. Annual.

Securities Industry Yearbook. New York: Securities Industry Association. Ranking of Securities Industry Association members by capital, number of offices, employees, and registered representatives. Major index alphabetical by firm also includes parent companies; major subsidiaries; number of offices, employees, and customer accounts; registered representatives; year founded; form of ownership; senior management and department heads; and capital position. Tables. Annual.

Standard & Poor's Security Dealers of North America. New York: Standard & Poor's Corporation. Brokers, distributors, dealers, and underwriters listed geographically and alphabetically. Data include officers, exchange and association membership, type of business, employer's industry number, and number of employees. A separate listing for foreign offices and representatives, new addresses, and discontinued firms. Semiannual.

Periodicals

The Asian Venture Capital Journal
Futures: The Magazine of Commodities and Options
Financial World
Going Public: The IPO Reporter
Institutional Investor
Investment Dealers' Digest
Journal of Business Venturing
Mergers & Acquisitions
Pensions & Investment Age
Venture Capital Journal
Worth

Compiled by: Sue Marsh
　　　　　　 Director, Current Collections Services
　　　　　　 Baker Library
　　　　　　 Harvard Business School